SUCCESS

ENGINEERING

IN A WORLD OF DISRUPTION

A Strategic Blueprint for Thriving in Uncertain Times

SHARESZ T. WILKINSON

USA TODAY AND WALL STREET JOURNAL
BESTSELLING AUTHOR

Leaders
Press

ISBN **978-1-63735-401-8** (pbk)
ISBN **978-1-63735-402-5** (hcv)
ISBN **978-1-63735-400-1** (ebook)

Library of Congress Control Number: **2025920872**

Contents

Introduction

1. Your New Life Starts Here

This book provides a compass on how to help you connect the dots. It is designed to inspire you to ask crucial life questions and help you gain clarity to bounce back fast when adversity strikes to engineer your successful outcomes with purpose.

This book teaches the discipline of the mind, followed by taking focused, conscious, and directed actions.

One arrow can only hit one target at a time. Focus on one chapter and one action at a time and make it happen. Take manageable steps, one day at a time, walking the path of your very own life journey and moving forward with focus.

With greater mental discipline, you are far more likely to prosper, lead a healthier life, and enjoy better relationships. Are you willing to put in the work? Dedicate yourself to progress and make strong self-leadership your sustainable default mode.

Strong self-leadership matters, not just for yourself. The changes it creates in you have a ripple effect.

By changing yourself, you change the people around you, leading by example. Incidentally, this is how true leadership works. There is no shortcut.

What we do daily matters, not just for ourselves, but for others as well and generations to come.

Fulfilled people tend to be happy, positive, and contribute to society.

"To act is to modify the world."
—Jean-Paul Sartre

To create a sustainable lifestyle, we need to reach awareness in the most relevant areas of life. We will look at what these are in more detail in this book.

Socrates asked to "Know Thyself." Know yourself; know the world. Self-knowledge is a powerful lifelong practice of discovery.

In this book, you will regularly assess a variety of metrics that will help you to understand yourself better, how you perform, and how to increase your outcomes substantially. You will be guided to take focused action and push ahead *effectively* to achieve your desired, best possible outcomes.

Every person is unique, which means that the best possible outcome will look different for each person!

Still, the process for achieving your goals remains the same.

By reading these pages and applying the methods step by step, you can powerfully overcome both professional and personal challenges.

Remember that creating the necessary self-awareness, revealing an ideal direction, and achieving clarity of purpose is a *process*. It takes time.

The only expert about your own life is you!

No one else knows your exact challenges, history, circumstances, dreams, aspirations, and wishes, as well as you do.

YOU are the expert of your own life!

The great news is that with this book, you can substantially increase your awareness and effectively work towards creating the outcomes you seek.

"Knowledge of mind and emotions should be taught in schools. On the basis of that understanding we can become healthy, happy individuals, families, communities, and societies. But if the mind is not disciplined, mere knowledge will not be of much help."
–Dalai Lama

2. Why Asking the Right Questions Is Important

Most people never really question themselves.
We often look for easy answers that come from the outside.

However, change starts with the questions we ask and answer ourselves from within.

Elon Musk once said that thinking of the right questions is the most difficult task.

Each chapter of this book removes that burden for you.

Instead of saying "Why me?!" when adversity strikes, asking these questions can revolutionize your attitudes, behavior, and most importantly, your outcomes.

Avoid branding yourself as a failure when things don't go your way.

Be kind and patient with yourself!

Instead, ask yourself why you do what you do. You may then find the answer. Here is an example: "Why do I always fail to stick to my projects until they are done?" Asking such a question, there *is* an answer, if he or she is totally honest in answering. Most often, fear is perceived as a massive block-age—fear of change, fear of success, fear of failure, fear of standing out.

The only certainties in life are uncertainty, change, and ulti-mately, death. Sometimes we realize this to a frightening degree.

However, the self-awareness we gain through asking the right questions and finding honest answers is priceless. It helps us successfully navigate life's uncertainties and chal-lenges and live more authentically, even joyfully.

Achieving self-awareness takes time. It can be challenging at times as the subconscious tries to block the changes we seek. Hence, it is crucial to work at your own speed. I don't recommend reading the whole book in one sitting. Your mind and emotional system could easily become overwhelmed. Break it down into manageable, sushi-sized portions.

Be kind to yourself! Take baby steps.

We, as humans, need time to grow and to change. A seed doesn't grow into a tree and bear fruit overnight. Patience!

Taking consistent daily actions, even small ones, adds up to big changes over time!

The key is to keep going. You have no choice as life continues either way.

This book is a manual and a compass that will guide you step by step. Its content is timeless, and will serve you well as a steady companion throughout your lifetime.

3. Find Your Mentors

"Very few highly resilient individuals are strong in and by themselves. You need support."
—Steven Southwick, Yale School of Medicine

Find someone ahead of you, someone who is where you want to be, and then adhere to their process. Invest the time, resources, and effort necessary to grow. Patience, grit, strong self-leadership, and perseverance are essential to personal growth and reaching our goals.

To substantially speed up this process, I suggest working with a professional. It is powerful to learn from the best experts you can afford, whether in finance, legal, health, or personal counsel.

As you grow, step by step, so too will the quality of your life, your networks, your resources, your health, and your success.

4. Mindset: How to Create Happiness

We are all on the same journey, discovering how to become fulfilled, while sitting together in the same rocky boat called life.

If we aim to create a better life for ourselves and our loved ones, no matter our culture, age, or background, we unite with humanity in its quest for love, acceptance, and inner peace, which are the key ingredients for happiness.

In nearly every instance, the key to unlocking what we want in life is a change in our mindset. Learning takes humility to be teachable and coachable. Focus on changing yourself, instead of others. This is the only area in life you truly can gain control over.

"Learning is a treasure that will follow its owner everywhere." –Chinese Proverb

Your personal growth and the development of strong self-leadership are substantial contributors to your happiness, fulfillment, prosperity, and success.

5. The Top 10 Workplace Skills

Here are the top 10 skills required in the workplace in the 21st century, according to the "Future of Jobs Report" by the World Economic Forum:

1. Complex problem-solving skills
2. Critical thinking
3. Creativity
4. People management
5. Coordinating with others
6. Emotional intelligence
7. Judgment and decision-making
8. Service orientation
9. Negotiation
10. Cognitive flexibility

All of these skills require self-awareness, an understanding of who we are and where we want to be.

Core skills expected to increase in importance by 2030 according to the latest report of the World Economic Forum are

1. AI and big data
2. Resilience, flexibility, and agility
3. Technological literacy
4. Creative thinking
5. Analytical thinking
6. Curiosity and lifelong learning
7. Leadership and social influence
8. Talent management

9. Motivation and self-awareness
10. Systems thinking
11. Empathy and active listening

Self-awareness and resilience can be engineered!

Let's dive right in and let's get started!

PART I

Your Story – The Master Key That Unlocks Your Life

---

1. We Define Ourselves by Our Stories

"You will never reach your destination if you stop and throw stones at every dog that barks."
–Winston Churchill

Our stories happened in the past. They are over and done, yet they form a big part of our present identities, and often our own misery.

Let us investigate why.

Sadness and hurt over the past drain a person's energy and headspace. These emotions absorb our current resources and our present time and focus. It is important to work through them. If necessary, with professional help in the case of trauma.

Why do we allow stories about the past to define who we are, and how we feel today?

1. We cannot change the past.
2. We cannot control what others think or do about the past.

To move forward, we will learn how to oversee our own minds and actions.

We can either ignore the painful stories in our heads (which are not going away), or we can retell them to our benefit from a more positive point of view.

The good news is that retelling works because stories are fluid.

Sounds like we have only one real option! So let us start with the story.

A person's story can be told in myriad negative or positive ways.

We will feel worse, or better, depending on how the story is told and what we focus on.

Brain imaging reveals that humans predominantly focus on bad memories. It seems we are hard-wired to recall mostly negative events, which is why it takes practice to override them.

Start with this realization:

> We are not our negative thoughts.
> Any negative memory is a one-sided story, there is more to it.

Why is the bad memory primary? The answer lies in our evolution. Focusing on the negative helped our survival as the human species. We would not have survived by recalling just the pretty sunsets, while forgetting about that man-eating saber-toothed tiger wanting to attack us. Remembering negative experiences kept and keeps humanity alive.

The fact that you're reading this means you've enjoyed a 100 percent survival rate so far, no matter what happened to you in life, in no small part thanks to uncomfortable memories.

What is real is our fear of what others think and might disapprove of, leading to being excluded from the group. This fear is very real. In early times, getting excluded from the tribe was a death sentence. Only being integrated into the group guaranteed survival, as a human could not survive alone. Our exclusion from the group meant certain death.

It goes without saying that the world has drastically changed since then.

Now, we can easily survive on our own, earn a living, and remain almost entirely independent from each other. However, psychologically, this fact has not caught up with our so-called reptilian brains. After thousands of years, we still feel intense fear over standing out and being excluded from our peers.

The problem is this programming, this subconscious survival behavior of focusing on the negative, blocks our best possible outcome.

This primal brain survival mechanism, the steady recollection of bad memories and possible dangers, is often not very helpful in achieving our goals and ambitions in present times.

The good news?

Once aware, we can learn how to consciously deal with our emotions and memories and focus on thoughts and relationships that move us forward.

"Eagles do not fly with ducks." –adapted from T. Harv Eker

2. How to Rewrite Your Story

At the very beginning of this process is *deciding* to use the positive parts of our stories and not focus on the negative parts.

This way we can achieve a positive mindset and outcome from our thoughts every day.

How can we achieve this?

Actively remember your successes, happy and proud moments, positive feedback, and outstanding experiences, from the very first memory forward.

Initially, this might take considerable effort until it becomes a habit!

Write these memories down because they are liable to slip from one's conscious mind. Keep your notes safe for future reference, particularly when you feel down, useless, or like being a failure.

It takes repetition and persistence to instill new and beneficial thinking patterns, which are strong enough to override our primordial instincts.

By doing this, it is possible to instill positive, constructive thoughts and emotions to influence you for the better.

Successful people cannot function with a mind filled with negativity. Focusing on the worst possible outcomes, even "just to be prepared," is a recipe for disaster, because the mind is so very powerful!

It has the capacity to create and attract whatever you put your energy and focus on!

You are the captain of your own ship!

Your very own thoughts create your daily actions and outcomes.

One disclaimer: Trauma triggers can create panic reactions that may feel paralyzing and which greatly inhibit clear thinking. If this happens, focus on breathing out longer than you breathe in until the trigger passes.

Although damaging, we often cling to drama and what feels safe and familiar even if we don't want to.

The survival kick of adrenaline and cortisol in a fear and stress response in the body can be highly addictive and damaging on a physical level.

Mentally, it can lead to a mindset filled with blame, anger, despair, and negativity; long term resulting in a victim mindset due to hopelessness and perceived helplessness. Trauma is deeply rooted. A qualified professional specialized trauma therapist can and will help through approaches such as EMDR and other types of therapy.

Coming back to the habitual negative thinking patterns, that we would like to change.

How can we steer the ship around?

3. Build a Happiness Habit

Positive affirmations and forced optimism alone don't work.

To do the inner work of gaining a genuinely positive perspective, regardless of how we currently feel, takes consistent daily action.

Building a happiness habit, especially with a brain naturally tuned for negativity in an unhappy and negative world, takes grit and making a daily decision.

No one jumps up this mountain.

Each day, reset your mind in the morning to create a habit of focusing on what you are grateful for.

We naturally resist and fear change. Transitions can be chaotic. Uncertainty is scary.

We fear the unknown, being empty-handed, and have a hard time holding the inner space for change to occur.

As an Asian saying goes: "The monkey who sticks his head out of the tree gets shot down first." So we think: Don't do it!

Familiar things, people, and circumstances appear to keep us safe. Fear inhibits us from standing out of the crowd or even making minor changes, trying to keep things at the status quo.

Yet what about public speaking, a promotion, life overseas, learning a new language and culture, starting your own business, or having to rebuild your life from scratch to survive in an ever faster changing world?

Learning how to overcome your fear of change and standing out plays a huge part in creating a successful journey.

In this book, we are going to learn how to do this. "Fear is a reaction. Courage is a decision."
–Sir Winston Churchill

Change is only possible for those ready to let go of old patterns and habits.

We need to let go of the victim mindset and take full accountability for ourselves to make our goals a reality!

4. What Do You Choose to Stand for?

In a first step toward reinvention, ask yourself:

Where do you want to go? What do you want to do? Who do you want to become? What do you choose to stand for?

Please answer these questions truthfully, and not based on convention, expectations, or what will make other people happy!

Living your own life and putting an end to people-pleasing is an excellent way to stop unnecessary suffering.

Why do we please others to our own detriment? No one else will suffer in our place.

It is time to see our own needs and wants as equally important!

They are the compass points, leading us to our own valuable decisions and destinations.

What do you have to offer to this world?

Think of it this way: we are all unique, there is only one 'you' in a world population of over 8 billion people!

Step into and own your space!

If you do not step into your space that is meant just for you, it cannot be filled by anyone else. You are unique for a reason.

You can't pour from an empty cup. It is only with a fulfilled life that you can truly make a difference, first to yourself , and then to each other.

"Give me a place to stand, and I can move the earth!"
–Archimedes

Health, success, and fulfillment are worth your time and effort to achieve, and it is possible for you to transform your awareness.

Like a butterfly, you can leave your caterpillar-self behind and transform inside and out.

You can grow wings, fly, and live your own life's purpose if you dare to do so.

This process might be the scariest of your life, but if you pull through it, it will give you the most beautiful outcome.

Nothing is more rewarding than creating the life you dream of.

It is not about where you start; it is about how you manage yourself moving forward, and where you finish!

"The first thing a great person does is make us realize the insignificance of circumstance."
–Ralph Waldo Emerson

Change creates chaos. It abolishes an old order, to establish a new one.

This fact is most likely the very reason, why we try to avoid it at all costs.

Yet the only way out is through!

How many times have people risen above difficulties to attain great success? From the ones that are loud and famous to the ones that are silent and private.

The greatest hero stories are those of an average person overcoming great challenges against all odds!

History is full of examples throughout the ages who have overcome tremendous hardships to reach victory and success.

Folk tales, movies, books, and inspirational videos build on such stories. So many celebrities have overcome great adversity.

For every celebrity who overcomes, countless others do the same day in and day out outside of the spotlight.

So why not you?

5. How Driven Are You?

Ask yourself:

- Am I driven by fear of loss, or by the excitement of creating new opportunities?
- Do I see my self, and behave, as a victim or a victor?
- Am I a passive follower, or a pro-active, self-driven doer?
- Is my life filled with new experiences and people? or are you a creature of old habits?

Most likely, the answer is a mix.

Emotions come and go like the weather.

They are the traffic signals of our soul. Fear means stop; pay attention, this is important!

We are not our emotions; we *have* them.

If you feel uneasy, angry, scared, or miserable about something, it is a very clear indication that something is off and deserves a closer look!

Observe, acknowledge, reflect, act, and let emotions pass just like the weather.

Instead of avoiding the topic or blaming yourself or others, unease and misery are strong signals that something is off and a change is needed!

Taking conscious actions takes courage and energy to protect your well-being!

Ask yourself:

- How bad must it get before I stand up for myself and the goals in my life?
- How much longer do I want to sacrifice my own health, well-being, sanity, resources, and happiness in an unhealthy situation?
- What values do I choose to teach my children about life, living them by example? Children learn predominantly from what they observe daily, not from what we tell them.

Show, do not tell! Model how good life can become with the necessary changes!

Focus on everything there is to gain with creativity, strength, and imagination.

Find the right people to support your quest.

If you can't get reliable, consistent, unbiased support, organize qualified professional help!

Change does not happen overnight. Friends and family are often the first ones to resist it heavily wanting you to stay the same, and where you are at!

At times, you must walk your way all by yourself for certain periods of time.

Constructive self-communication and learning how to calm your negative inner voices are critical.

6. Learning How to Improve Your Self-Communication

Proper self-communication is essential for creating positive change.

When you learn how to reduce the negative self-talk in your head, you set the course of your life in a very specific and consciously chosen direction. You move forward to engineer your own success.

6.1 Curate Your Own Thoughts

Make sure your thoughts focus on and create your most desirable future!

The awareness of how you think directly determines your life's direction and outcome.

We can create our own circumstances.

Take responsibility and accountability for the quality of your thoughts.

Who we become and what we do is ultimately directed by our self-communication, and our daily choices. Own them!

"I am neither embarrassed of who I am, where I come from, what I have experienced. This is actually who I am."
–Shania Twain

6.2 How to Choose Your Best Possible Outcome

How can we create this thought-awareness and change our focus and actions toward what we want to achieve on a consistent basis?

Here is an efficient way to do this:

Physically write down your best possible outcome on paper.
Focus on the what and by when, not on the how! Write in the present, 'I am/We are...', 'I/We have...' Do not censor your own thought process!

Do this every day for five minutes in the morning.
It does not matter if you repeat yourself.

Keep the paper with you as your personal compass for decision making.

This will help to ask yourself regularly:
Does this decision/action/person/behavior

- Lead me towards or away from my best possible outcome?
- Help me build a clear focus, goal, and purpose?
- Set healthy boundaries?
- Assert and say "No" to things and people that lead away from my goals and values?
- Take actions that lead me toward my goals?
- Helps me stay the course until success is achieved?

Ask for What You Want!

People cannot read your mind. Writing down your goals daily will give you a clear compass, helping you gain clarity and seize opportunities.

Dare to ask. Remember that it is a numbers game.

There are only two possible outcomes, yes or no. In which case, you are in the same position as you are now. A yes can change everything!

We can improve our negotiation and communication skills through practice.

The more you learn how to assert yourself, the more your success rate will go up.

Slowly, over time, you will steer your life-ship in the direction of your ultimate goals and purpose.

6.3 Family Roots: The Foundation from Which We Grow Into Our Own Selves

Have you ever wondered: "How free am I, really, in my own decisions?"

We often want or tend to ignore our ancestry, or we simply do not know about it anymore, especially in Western countries.

Yet not one single person is an island and exists by and through themselves.

Here is the bad news: if we are not aware of our family's past, we are bound to unknowingly repeat negative patterns and behaviors.

Once we learn about the history, fates, and tragedies within our family history over previous generations, we become much more aware of where we are repeating patterns and challenges.

This knowledge serves very much like a medical family history.

It is highly relevant to consider this when we hit a wall in life, and despite trying everything, cannot seem to over-come it.

The relevant work starts with us: our personal histories, and the tales of our families.

Who Are You?
Learn as much as you can about:

- Your geographical origins (there are DNA tests and ancestry research databases available)
- Your family background
- Your family history
- The Fates of your family members. What happened to them?
  How did they pass on?

Learn as much as you can up to the grandparents on both sides, including siblings, uncles, and aunts if possible!

It does take persistent research and honest conversations.

It is a great opportunity as it leads to much more authentic relationships.

Sometimes, we must pull the skeletons out of the closet to get to the truth.

The more you learn, the better your understanding of yourself.

Find out about:

- Who had similar traits as me?
- Whose history is like mine? Are patterns repeating themselves over generations?
- Which thoughts and behaviors have I taken over unknowingly?

- What are the hidden secrets of my family history? Who is missing in it and why? What happened to certain family members? How did they pass away? Were there hidden tragedies, losses, shame, guilt, and difficulties that I now carry?
- What are the victories, achievements, successes, big wins, and life-changing decisions that carried my family forward, maybe over generations?

First, this crucial information will make a lot of traits more conscious in your personal identity.

It sheds light on roots and a more accurate understanding of yourself and your background, and even if one never met the members of their ancestry in person, it leads to a much stronger sense of identity and belonging. These are your roots.

"No roots, no wings." –Ghanaian saying

Second, do not focus on *why* people did what they did. It is history.
Only focus on what WAS.

Acceptance of what happened is the key to one's peace and inner freedom, as we cannot change it! This takes time and practice working through your own emotions.

As each of us ages and gains in understanding and wisdom, we see new insights emerge from old facts, and more puzzle pieces starting to fit together.

Third, now that the family history is better known, you can answer these questions:

- Which thought patterns are truly my very own, and which ones did I take over, follow, or embody (from others or society) without much conscious reflection or thought?
- Which beliefs do I want to keep in my life? What is true for me today?
- Are there certain patterns, habits, thoughts, and behaviors, that are not really mine, which I am ready to let go of consciously now?

Once aware, we can start to change.

Once you know the "what," you can then strategize "how" you personally want to live and follow up with taking conscious actions in that direction.

6.4 What Will You Change?

If your life depended on it, and it does! What would you change right now?

Again, keep in mind that you cannot change other people, only yourself!

Whatever stories you repeatedly tell yourself , they define your day-to- day life, and the outcome!

We are usually hardest on ourselves, so the stories we often recall are about how we fail, including how we are "failures" in one way or another.

We naturally remember our failings much more than our victories and good character traits.

Recall your strengths and your victories! Write them all down!

This process allows you to become easier on and kinder to yourself!

The brain *can* be 'rewired'. Our memories *can* be reframed through a conscious change in our thinking patterns.

It takes practice to physically create new pathways of thinking in the brain, but it is achievable over time.

Here are the steps again in summary:

- **Step 1**: We can actively remember all our victories, successes, and positive memories. Refresh your memory with photos, awards, and mementos and by asking your friends and relatives for their positive memories about you.
- **Step 2:** Write your best possible outcome every day! Do it first thing in the morning.
  This sets your inner compass in the right direction.
  Note: Over time, your daily outcome will change and become more detailed. Be very precise about what you really want!
- **Step 3:** Make it a non-negotiable to celebrate successes and reward yourself after reaching each milestone!
  Do the same with and for your loved ones.

These are potent steps, and you will notice a considerable change in your thinking, as well as in your life. You create and attract what you focus on.

When we are in it, change occurs at a seemingly annoying snail's pace!

Yet in hindsight, we will be amazed at the massive changes created in just a few months or one year!

Stay the course and take action toward your goals daily!

Patience, focus, grit, and perseverance will get you virtually anywhere in life.

"Success is not final; failure is not fatal: it is the courage to continue that counts."
–Winston Churchill

Be Aware

Once we change something, the people in our lives, and even our surroundings or circumstances, will often desperately try to change us back into how we used to be!

People feel uncomfortable with our changes, and try to push our victories out of their comfort zones.

Familiar patterns die hard. Do not give in to the pressure of the familiar and stay the course.

Many of your negative and repeating thoughts are responses heard or designed by your much younger self for survival.

The self as a young child did not know how to cope. It was over whelmed and had no power or means. A young child can not change or leave its immediate environment.

As an adult, it is a mature step to examine these thoughts and feelings, as you now DO have the power and the choice to change them .

If you cannot manage to do so despite consistent efforts, please seek help from a professional psychologist or therapist.

An old Cherokee grandfather is telling his grandson a story. "A fight is going on inside me," he said. "A terrible fight between two wolves. One is evil. He has anger, envy, greed, arrogance, resentment, lies, and ego. "The other one is good. He has joy, peace, love, hope, serenity, humility, kindness, empathy, generosity, truth, compassion, and faith. It is a fight to the death."

Wide-eyed, the boy asks which wolf wins.

His grandfather softly says, "The one you feed."

7. Key Questions to Ask About Your Story

- What is my story?
- How do I see and describe myself?
- Is this my own belief, or did I take it over, embody, or follow it from someone else?
- Who has said such things to me?
- How old was I when I remember the earliest incident relating to this thought or feeling?

- When did they say this? What were the outer circumstances?
- How long have I been carrying this belief around with me?
- Do I want to carry this belief forward, or rather not? Is it still relevant to me?
- If not, can I forgive and let go for my own sake? Ask yourself: Could I let it go? Would I let it go? If yes, when will I let it go? Then, make that decision and stick to it.
- Focus on your successes and rewrite your story in a positive light!

Life looks so beautiful and seemingly easy in the spotlight or when we are on a roll. If you do not know anything about your biological family roots, and many do not, find knowledge in the history of your place or culture of origin, and see what resonates within you.

Few see the blood, sweat, and tears, the delayed gratification and focus, often over decades, that lead to the glorious moments and acknowledgments in life, our successes.

When anyone puts you down, says you have had it easy, or tries to belittle you and your dreams, save your energy. Smile graciously and move on!

Continue to take focused action to achieve goals steadily over time instead of disputing the perceptions and opinions of other people, which is a futile endeavor.
Focus on your own journey instead.

Your future success will prove them wrong. . .you have to believe in yourself first!

You are the expert in your own life, and you can find all the answers within.

As you start to turn down the volume of negative thinking, you begin to listen to yourself and your intuition and focus on your best possible outcome!

8. Moving Forward Into Empowered Thinking

The real question now is *how* to connect the dots of to-dos and laser focus on the outcome. How do we propel ourselves forward?

Gather the Facts First.

Knowledge is power. It creates a roadmap, and the ability to see the bigger picture. It helps to identify the gaps in what we need to work on.

Take consistent action and create confidence as you start to build momentum.

Momentum creates more successful experiences and brings results.

Awareness is key in pushing us towards the goals we want to achieve: better relationships, a higher paying job or more fulfilling work, more opportunities, reaching our dreams and aspirations, and taking care of our health and well-being.

"When the light comes, darkness cannot prevail." –Anonymous

When you are aware of who you are, where you came from, and what you want, you are now able to set your life's course in the direction that you truly want to go in!

What do you choose to stand for?

It is now a conscious choice, and an exciting journey lies ahead!

Recognize your strengths, gifts, talents, and calling .

Your intrinsic value cannot be damaged, altered, or destroyed. We all have value. We are each born with it: our value is innate. It cannot be damaged, transferred to another, or lost.

9. How to Spring Clean Your Life

Analyze, detox, and declutter the parts of your life that hold you back. Think it through step by step, followed by taking focused action, and you will have the opportunity to Optimize your:

- Lifestyle
- Relationships
- Health
- Diet
- Living environment
- Language
- Mind
- Work
- Structures
- Finances

Get rid of or transform the old that does not serve you any longer to create space for the new!

This will greatly help you become who you really want to be and achieve your goals.

Circumstances change constantly. Life is changing fast, and we need to keep up and adapt if we want to stay relevant.

Maintaining or regaining our **health**, **well-being**, and **happiness** is the foundation. They determine how well we adapt to the challenges. Life throws curve balls at us as long as we live.

Fighting change is therefore a waste of time. Go with it and learn how to surf the waves.

Acceptance is key to resilience and bouncing back fast from difficulties and setbacks.

Create a solid compass to steer and keep your life ship on course even in rough waters.

There's no need to do it all alone.

Asking for help if and where required is a sign of intelligence and strength!

Start by asking *yourself first* the following questions to create an uncensored vision of your life:

1. How and where do you want to live?

2. What do you want to do?
3. Who do you want to be or become?
4. What do you choose to stand for?
5. For whom or what?
6. Why?
7. By when?

Now that you have a first iteration of your vision, notice the gap between where you are *now* and where you want to be in the future.

Research in as detailed a way as possible:

What action steps are required to get where I want to be? What is the next easiest step I need to take to get there?

Start with the easiest task(s) first. Then tackle the next, and so on. One by one.

As an Asian saying goes, "Mountains are built pebble by pebble."

Gather *facts, figures,* and *to-dos*.

You are not making assumptions, and you are not allowing your vision to remain a dream. You are now working to make it a reality by writing and speaking about it.

This is a very powerful process!

Ask professionals for help in relevant areas. Use online tools to do your research.

If you want to succeed, avoid asking family and friends for advice as they are biased and not neutral.

Most often, they are not qualified to provide professional information!

Do your research online, and always verify information at source, not through third parties.

Work whenever possible with the best professionals or tools you can afford.

A dream is great. It is where everyone starts.

But ideas are cheap if they are not put into action steps and followed through to completion.

Once you add facts, figures, steps, and a deadline to a vision, you have created a solid action plan to create your new reality!

You are creating your own new life and taking accountability for it.

Every day, you create your life with your own thoughts, decisions, and actions. Focus on the meaningful goals you want to achieve.

This allows you to unclutter and frees tremendous space and precious energy.

Most importantly, this will allow you to overcome the fear of letting go of what is obsolete and the negative and make continuous progress toward achieving your dreams.

"The key to growth is the introduction of higher dimensions of consciousness into our awareness." –Lao Tzu

What You Need to Know

We each have Six Human Needs, according to Abraham Maslow and outlined by Anthony Robbins, which are important for our self-actualization.

These needs are non-negotiable.

That means if any one of these six needs is out of balance or unmet, we *will* naturally strive to find what we are missing in our current circumstances or relationships.

The six human needs, according to Tony Robbins, are:

1. **Certainty** - the assurance that one can avoid pain and gain pleasure.
2. **Uncertainty / Variety** - the need for new stimuli, the unknown and change.
3. **Significance** - the need for feeling unique, important, needed, or special.
4. **Connection / Love** - a strong feeling of closeness or union with someone or something.
5. **Growth** - the need for expansion of capacity, capability, or understanding.
6. **Contribution** - a sense of service and focus on helping, giving to, and supporting others

Which of these needs are not fully met in your life? How can you fulfill them in healthy ways to become more balanced?

Keep the Six Human Needs in mind when dealing with *other* people! You will be able to relate to them in a much more comprehensive and empathetic manner .Ask yourself: Which of their needs are most likely not met in any given situation?

You will become a more empathetic communicator, observing and genuinely listening to others.

These six needs offer us invaluable access to a different perspective in understanding ourselves and others better.

Think of the Six Human Needs first in your own life, and ask yourself the following questions:

Where are shortcomings?
How can I begin to remedy them?
Where do I feel uncomfortable in my life?

In which areas of my life am I happy and content? In which do I feel unhappy, or even resentful?

What about my partner, my children, my friend, my colleague, or my boss?

The six areas seem to be of equal importance because we are all holistic beings.

They underinvest in the areas they are weak in, such as relationships or giving back.

They overinvest in the areas they are strong in, such as health or money.

Most people do not invest equitably across the different facets of their lives: They underinvest in the areas they are weak in. They overinvest in the areas they are strong in.

It is a vicious cycle: Underinvesting in one domain robs you of your wholeness. The loss bleeds out into the rest of your life.

This will cause you to compensate and overinvest in just one or two parts, which shifts your approach from living fully to one of damage control.

While working in South Africa years ago, a businessman approached me after a public speaking event. He looked miserable and confused. I asked if he was okay. He said no. "What happened?" I asked.

He said: "I put all my money into a startup business, and it went belly up. I lost everything."

It is very distressing to lose your business, and he was completely crushed. He defined his identity solely through career success and money. Devastated, he felt his life was over and meaningless because of this failure. He was suicidal.

"Are you married?" I asked. "Yes," he said. "Do you love your wife?" "Yes."

"Do you have a good relationship with your children?" "Yes."

"Are you and your family members healthy?" "Yes, we are healthy," he agreed.

"Do you still have food on the table? Clothes on your bodies? And a roof your heads?"

"Yes!"

Relentlessly, and quickly, I questioned him on the eight relevant life areas we are going to cover in the second part of this book.

He lacked (temporarily) success in but two out of eight areas: Business and Finance.

But he enjoyed six equally important areas, in which he succeeded better than the average person!

When I made him aware of this and explained the eight areas in life, he realized how fortunate he really was. He also understood that compared to the difficulty of finding a loving, longterm relationship or building a happy marriage, money can be relatively quickly remade with the proper knowledge and skills that he can work and improve on.

I assuaged his loss by mentioning that I have yet to meet any adult who has never lost any money in business or through some other financial mishap or bad decision. Losing money shows that you are *in the game*. It is simply the other side of the coin of success.

The key lies in dusting yourself off, getting back into the saddle so to speak, and to keep going, learning, and improving.

However, he was oblivious to this process. He was in too much pain, because his fear of being a complete failure and losing everything had kept him emotionally *paralyzed* and depressed at a time when he needed all his energy and strength to focus on solutions!

Those twenty minutes of profound insight turned his life around.

He cut his losses. He learned from it. He moved on. One year later, he sent me updates and photos of his family, and they were prospering again.

If we learn how to reframe our mindset and override the physical stress response, we can walk away from fear. When we are afraid, we must remember this very true saying:

"Fear kills quicker than a weapon."

10. Learning How to Overcome Your Fear Is Crucial to Reaching Your Goals

"Everything we want is on the other side of fear." —Jack Canfield

Faced with a threat to one of your essential needs in life, you are likely going to feel afraid, just as this (temporarily) failed businessman did in South Africa.

We only fail if we give up and quit.

Having a family, as in his case, giving up is not an option! Fear is the biggest roadblock in most people's lives.

Your silent everyday sellouts and missing out on your biggest victories are both caused by fear. Often over-whelming fear.

How do you lose out being afraid?

When you are not in the present moment, it is easy to get stuck thinking too far ahead or too far back.

When you are fearful, you become paralyzed in your mind, body, and actions. Overthinking can paralyze you and guar-antee your most feared outcome coming true!

1. You are focusing on it to the exclusion of all else.
2. You are not taking any positive action and procrastinating!

How can we turn this fear into action? First, notice that you are afraid!

Again, awareness is the first step to change.

What Fear Feels Like

You might notice an uneasy feeling in the belly or having a knot in your stomach. You will feel nervous and restless, and you might start thinking frantically, as if your brain is running in circles to find a solution.

1. If you are afraid, you might sweat and feel tense this is your body's "fight" response.
2. You might feel stuck, on edge, nervous, and unable to think clearly, this is your body's "flight" response.

You might start to mirror your perceived threat's behavior to people please, this is your body's "fawn" response.

3. Or you might feel numbed out, and distract yourself as much as possible, hoping it will blow over or go away somehow this is your body's "freeze" response.

To numb yourself, you might use and compensate with food, work, sports, binge-watching , endless scrolling, gambling, drinking, drugs, sex, social media, playing with danger, and the like, leading to severe self-sabotage and addictions.

We blank out instead of directly facing our overwhelming emotions and actively working through them

The only way out is through.

How do *you* react when you are afraid?

The beginning of courage is getting to know your telltale symptoms of reacting to fear and triggers to recognize what is going on.

We can't change what we are not aware of.

The most important thing when we face a challenge is to realize how we deal with our own FEAR.

The fear of failure, of not being good enough, irrelevant, of loss or not being able to provide, the fear of not being healthy, personal anxiety, and of things that and events that are beyond our control.

Although these concerns might be real, most of the time our thinking is clouded by worries, remaining waiting and passive.

Worries are like a rocking chair that keeps us busy but does not get us anywhere!

Yet fear has its place. Reasonable fear is healthy and keeps us safe. It calls attention to an urgent issue.

Unreasonable, debilitating fear is unhealthy and hurts you in the long run.

When fear tells you that an important issue needs your attention *immediately*, acknowledge this feeling, pay attention, and minimize your reaction through the 3-minute breathing exercise described below in detail.

Then, take focused action, starting with the easiest one first. The fear will subside!

Learn how to do things afraid. Overriding the fear response in the body allows you to become able to move forward.

The moment you act, fear tends to disappear as its purpose has been fulfilled calling attention to an important issue that needs to be addressed now.

Here are four points to keep in mind when dealing with fear:

1. **Fear ignites an immediate flight, fight, freeze, or fawn response in your body.**

If you react to the situations that you encounter, you are giving away your power.

To keep your power, which is a clear mind and self-control, practice being present, even during challenging moments. Pay attention, and face the fear.

Being present means remaining open and non-judgmental: observing and listening honestly, without reservation, and accepting what really *IS*.

Easier said than done.

Here is how: first, you will need to calm your nervous system to think clearly.

Powerful Breathing Technique

The following **3-minute** technique helps you create inner calm quickly by focusing on counting your breath.

You might say: I know this one from meditation or Yoga.

Not quite it is used in the military.

This exercise helps army professionals being able to stay focused and think clearly before going into action.

They conciously calm down their nervous system in just under 3 minutes.

Do this breathing exercise daily.

Your body will create a habitual response and be able to change into a calm state immediately due to practice and body memory.

Breathe consciously, with complete focus, for three minutes.

Keep breathing and body posture normal; there is no need to close your eyes.

Why is this focused, deep breathing exercise so helpful and powerful?

It detaches you emotionally from your current circumstances and calms your nervous system down, no matter what is going on around you.

It is a great tool to center yourself immediately in times of stress, emergencies, or when you have to make important decisions under high pressure. Breathe in for 3 seconds, and out for 4 seconds anywhere and at any time.

Do not be afraid to take this quick time out.

Excuse yourself for a few minutes if needed, go to a quiet place (the bathroom will do) and fully focus on this breathing technique.

You can even do this exercise discreetly and unknown to others during meetings.

Research has shown that breathing this way instantly calms down your body and mind.

You will quickly become rooted, grounded and calm, even in highly stressful situations!

Breathe.

Focus! Keep going one step at a time.

Now you have a simple, highly effective, and efficient tool available.

It provides you with inner space to think clearly, make better decisions, and focus on taking one action step at a time.

Practice daily so your body will quickly remember it in stressful situations.

2. **Fear is a lifesaver. It warns you when things are important and need your attention now!**
    Keep in mind: *It is extremely rare to be in a truly life-threatening situation in the very moment.*

If you are breathing and safe, there is nothing to fear! Everything will eventually get sorted out over time. Remind yourself of these facts.

Breathing is essential to life. Without breath, we die in minutes.

If you are breathing, you are okay. Take it one moment at a time.

You only ever must make it through the next one minute at a time! Focus on this.

3. **Fear is an important signal that you need to pay attention to immediately.**

How do we process the fear that remains? Use these feelings to spur *action*. This is how we grow, by taking massive action that stretches us past our points of comfort.

Tackle taxing situations ONE step at a time.

Compartmentalize problems:

Handle ONE action to solve ONE problem at a time, right NOW.

Start with the easiest one to solve and work your way through it. Then tackle the next one and so forth, step by step, building your momentum.

Breathe. Focus. Stay in the present moment. Do not stress about the rest.

People can survive incredible pain and difficulties by staying in the moment.

We cannot always change circumstances, the external triggers.

But **we can strive to change our reactions to it**! *"Do or do not. There is no try."* –Yoda

We can shift from *victim* to *victor*, taking conscious, focused action to keep our emotions in check and deal with facts and figures instead of fear.

Remember, emotions are fickle! They constantly change.

One moment you can be happy; the next, you can be afraid, angry, bored or even a mix of several emotions at once. They come and go. The fastest way to deal with them is to feel them, acknowledge them, and let them pass. Suppression and denial store emotions in our bodies and lead to all sorts of undesirable health and psychological issues down the line.

Stay focused on what you want to accomplish. Again, you are not your emotions; you have them!

Over time, you can become proficient in handling your emotions in a healthier manner.

Enjoy the good ones and *let* the bad ones pass.

Do not avoid them; hold onto them, but focus on what you want to *do* and get it done regardless of how you feel. Take a breath , but then get back into the saddle, so to speak.

Be kind to yourself in this process.

4. **Take charge, despite your fear, and rise to meet the challenge.**
Fear is a cousin to procrastination.

They both lead to stress, anxiety, blocked progress, and over-whelm. Their destructive patterns erode not only your effi-ciency, results, and progress but also your self-confidence.

Practice the three-minute breathing exercise daily!

It is powerful and will reliably give you a grasp on your emotions and your mind.

If a situation is too overwhelming, no matter what you do, please get help.

Hire a professional to help you deal with a specific situation.

Look for a qualified professional coach, counselor, psychologist, or psychotherapist with whom you can easily relate.

Many online platforms offer inexpensive counseling.

Read books. Watch videos. Listen to podcasts and audiobooks.

There is a huge number of online resources available to help you work through personal challenges. Then there is the one timeless, *internal* media:

Pray, if it is within you.

Turning to prayer has helped many in the most difficult situations, unleashing a hidden power within.

Bear in mind that without you taking massive action, your efforts, both internal and external, will not bear the results that you are looking for.

There is no shortcut to success.

You must put in the work with consistency.

At no stage in human history has information been so easily and readily accessible.

Today, we do not have any excuse to remain imprisoned in a narrow mindset with emotional suffering. The internet and AI have democratized knowledge and intelligence, the power of outreach and communication.

They allow us to keep learning, connecting, and growing within the comfort and safety of our own four walls.

Free support groups and online chat forums encourage you to share your experiences with like-minded group members all over the world: research posts, articles, and videos on your topics. If there are toxic participants or comments, it has never been so easy to delete and block them. You are in charge and literally create your own environment!

Courage is taking action, despite having fears.

"You cannot build a reputation on what you are going to do."
–Henry Ford

Reframe FEAR to *False Evidence Appearing Real* and *Face Everything and Rise!* Everything you want is on the other side of fear.

Get started. Learn to take action when you are afraid!

11. How to Create Clarity in the Present

"You were born to win, but to be a winner, you must plan to win, prepare to win, and expect to win." –Zig Ziglar

Your mind cannot focus on two things at once! We can only have one thought at a time.

There is no capacity to think about anything else. So, be very selective about which thoughts you choose to focus on!

How to direct your thoughts to the present moment? The breathing exercise is one powerful technique.

Another one is to use all your senses to realize all that is going on around you right now. Sight, touch, taste, smell, hearing, movement.

Add your gut instinct; listen to it. It is never wrong.

Assess each sense:

> What do you see around you? What do you physically feel? What is the taste in your mouth? What can you smell?
> What sounds do you hear?
> Where and how is your body in this very space? What does your gut say?

The present moment is all we ever have!
The past is gone; it cannot be changed, only accepted. The future has not yet arrived.

What reality do you choose to create?

If you learn how to become present in this very moment with all your being, a couple of things will happen:

You will feel a sense of awe, then gratitude, joy and a growing curiosity about life.

If you manage to get out of your head, and into the present moment, you will start noticing all the little things you otherwise don't notice.

Life will become so much more enjoyable and joyful.

If you are pushing and forcing a goal relentlessly, with all your strength, this often will *not* lead you to get what you want.

However, what it *will* create is a lot of tension, stress, and frustration.

Be patient. Relax and learn to let go after the effort is done, very much like an archer shooting an arrow to hit the bullseye of the target.

Strive to keep a balance to meet all your needs. Flowers don't grow faster by pulling on their heads!

The point is, we must make time for ourselves, especially during our bad times.

We can only change what we are aware of. Pay attention to how you feel and when things are off. Strive to set them right.

The importance of intentional doing, giving our very best, and *then letting go*, detaching ourselves *emotionally* from the outcome, helps to keep our inner balance and sanity.

After maximum effort, you allow things to fall into place after giving your best. Trust in the process, life, and yourself. Hold the mental space to consistently focus on your best possible outcome.

"When you stand with your two feet on the ground, you will always keep your balance." —Taoist proverb

Are you dysfunctional with an inclination for drama? If this is the case for you, know that you are going to attract more of the same thing that you are focusing on!

The same type of people. The same type of circumstances. The same type of experiences.

Hence, watch your mind and your thoughts!

Focus on what you want!

Remember: Instead of blaming and trying to change others, your energy and resources are much better deployed on what you *do* have control over, which is changing yourself and your circumstances toward what you want to create for yourself moving forward in your life.

Become the person you want to be with.

You spend more time with yourself than anyone else from the cradle to the grave!

We come alone with nothing, and we will leave alone with nothing.

Learning how to enjoy the various stages in life is key.

"If you want a certain thing, first be a certain person. Then, obtaining that certain thing will no longer be a concern."
–Zen Proverb

To attract positive and great events into our life, we must become positive and great in our own right. We have to step up to our own expectations.

Ask yourself the following questions:

- Am I reliable, accountable, and dependable?
- Have I developed a positive attitude and a sense of gratitude?
- Am I adaptable and honest?
- Do I act with integrity?
- Am I who I want to be?
- Am I self-motivated to learn and grow?
- Do I strive to be professional and ethical with others?
- Do I enforce healthy boundaries and keep drama out of my life?
- Do I take care of my health, appearance, and well-being?

The more positive answers you have, the more likely you are to attract positive people and experiences.

Our attitudes, mindset, appearance, lifestyle, down to how we carry ourselves and communicate, these can all be refined to get us where we want to be.

"A diamond is a piece of coal that did well under pressure."
–Henry Kissinger

If the coal would complain every time it is cut, shaped, and polished, there would be no sparkling diamonds.

12. Highly Effective Problem-Solving Tools

To effectively analyze a situation, focus on the *facts* first, without getting carried away by your emotions. Breathe and think. *Assumptions are not facts*. You cannot take assumptions into consideration when you are analyzing a problem to make an important decision.

Strategize the required steps that you need to take towards achieving a realistic solution; dealing with what *is*. Overthinking stems from not taking action, and using these wobbly words: wish, could, should, nobody, everybody, never, and always.

Instead of worrying about a challenge, think about what steps to take to rise to it. This empowers you and puts you fair and square back into the driver's seat of your life.

Sometimes, you are going to find yourself in a heated situation.

We are not always able to avoid conflict and emotional upheaval, especially if the other person is bound to it.

You will find the root cause of a challenge ONLY by avoiding these words:

Nobody
Everybody
Always

Never
Should
Could
Would
If
Try (implies failure)
Nothing
Everything
Nowhere
Everywhere

These words are misleading absolutes, which arise when you are feeling emotional. They are wishy-washy, provocative, and non-committal.

These words create false perceptions, make assumptions, imply blame, guilt, and shame, and impose needless pressure.

Avoid creating misunderstandings and walls. However, it is hard to speak without them! It will take your awareness and practice to consciously rid them of your communication.

Do step away from a conflict and take a time out if the other person or you are incapable of adhering to human decency and even the most basic respect.

Losing face over a few words said in great anger creates tremendous havoc and irreparable damage to relationships.

If it ever does happen, apologize properly, and please mean it!

When you are angry, stuck, worried, or stressed:

1. Take a time out; go for a walk.
2. First and foremost, focus on yourself at that moment. You do not need the circumstances or the other person to change to gain clarity, because only you can change yourself and your life!
3. Calm your mind with the breathing exercise.
4. When you need to think of a solution, the next step or a way out, start answering the 10 questions mentioned below. Be logical. Be a detective: Focus on facts!
5. Strive not to accuse, deny, blame, project, or provoke, neither yourself nor others. Remember that people think and speak *from their very own* perspective and experience, not yours! How people behave tells you more about them than about yourself.

Decide on the most reasonable, healthy, and constructive thing you can do in any given situation.

Sharesz T. Wilkinson's 10 Questions Framework

Answering the following 10 questions regarding challenges, or any situation creates the greatest *clarity*.

Analyzing a situation in this manner helps us to define what can be done about it.

If you need more information or guidance, do your research and ask professionals to help define your next steps of action. Come prepared, with all the data you have gleaned from answering the Ten Questions.

This framework will lead to incredibly productive conversations and problem-solving skills!

Ask yourself these

Ten Questions to Get to the Root of Any Challenge

- Who?
- What?
- When?
- Where?
- With whom?
- How?
- How long?
- How much/how many?
- Why?
- What is next?

Continue to ask these questions adapted to a specific situation until you get to the root cause of an issue.

The one thing necessary for success is that you give and get honest answers.

Without honest answers, you will keep looking for solutions in all the wrong places!

Here is an example that will help to understand the process better:

Who is involved? What happens? When does it occur? Where does it take place? With whom does it take place? How do we make it happen? How long does it take? How much (resources, money, effort) does it take? How many people are involved? Why do we want to do this in the first place? What is our next course of action?

You can also use this to analyze and communicate meetings prior to scheduling to make things a lot more effective and efficient.

Further, **before** you deal with any problem or situation, ask yourself:

— Am I able to change something here, or not?

Is changing anything here within my level of authority, reach and capability? If the answer is yes, then the next question is:

— Do I **want** to do something about it?

What does it cost in time, energy, reputation, money, and relationships? Are you willing to make this effort? Yes, or no?

Then, take a conscious decision and choose a course of action.

How to Let Go of the Negative and Forge Ahead

Usually, the only person to suffer from carrying negative emotions and memories is yourself!

We punish ourselves and prolong our own suffering unnecessarily, often across decades, by holding on to grudges, resentments, and even hatred.

The other person involved has probably moved on long ago or is not even aware of how you feel about it! They might even have *passed away* in the meantime! They also may think of the grievances very differently and not feel a drop of what you are experiencing.

That is why having a vengeful mind is like drinking poison… and hoping the other person is going to perish!

Your job is to oversee yourself and how you react to your own thoughts.

> You are *not* in charge of *other people's* thoughts or behavior.

How can you have control over another mind?

Think about how hard it is to navigate your very own mind! "Not my monkeys, not my circus." serves as a very good reminder to respect boundaries, our own and others' if you are worried about what others might think.

People are usually way too busy thinking about themselves and their own daily lives and challenges. Not about you.

Suddenly you might feel like being in a vacuum.

When we no longer focus on others and our attention going to blame, anger, and shaming others, but on ourselves, THIS is the beginning of our real responsibility: striving to fill the void with the real you unapologetically.

What do you want to create in your life?

Minding our own business is a 24/7 full-time job!

To let go requires great strength, maturity, and forgiveness.

"The weak can never forgive. Forgiveness is the attribute of the strong." –Mahatma Gandhi

It is far from being a weakness; it is a superpower! It harnesses energy for your more constructive and beneficial endeavors.

Acceptance does not mean approval of what happened it frees you from the emotional cage caused by what hurt you.

Consider that most people are doing the best they can with who they are and where they are at, given their specific circumstances, even if it does not look like it.

Freeing yourself from those negative feelings is powerful.

You are only ever one choice away from a totally different lifestyle!

All it takes is making the one decision and then following through with taking solid actions.

It takes humility to admit that no one is perfect, us included!

So busy with our own emotions and lives, we make mistakes, often unaware of how those decisions impact other people, and even more unaware of how they impact us.

Move despite the fear and create positive outcomes by focusing on the next step, growth, learning, and moving forward.

Brush three things every day: your teeth, your hair, and the chips off your shoulder!

Past experiences do not live on unless we keep them alive in our memory and regularly revisit them!

This is a very unhealthy habit.

The pain experienced when we recall difficult situations is self-inflicted. Develop the discipline to focus forward and on positive outcomes.

"The secret of change is to focus all of your energy, not on fighting the old, but on building the new."
—Socrates

> Ask yourself
> What is it that I love to do?
> What makes me happy and fulfilled?
> What did I enjoy doing in my youth and as a child? What were the experiences that lit me up?
> Which innate talents do I have that lay unused and forgotten?

Finding these points and making them a part of your life again, and on a regular basis, can revive your joy and happiness to lighten up!

Taking yourself and life less seriously is a great way to be more joyful. We never get back the time we spend!

Use it wisely and without regret.

Find opportunities and circumstances to bring play and fun back into your routine.

Life is short. Make it memorable and enjoyable; it is your very own responsibility. This awareness is crucial to a happy and fulfilled lifestyle.

"Whether you think you can, or you think you cannot you are right!"
–Henry Ford

How to Lose with Style

Change is hard. It rarely happens on your preferred schedule. You cannot always win. Failing faster leads inevitably to greater success!

That is why it is *crucial* to *learn how to lose gracefully*, to let go quickly, and to be able to learn some hard lessons without getting worked up over what you cannot change.

These include both circumstances (and people) who are bigger than you can handle. There is no such thing as instant success, no matter what social media or influencers tell us.

We need *grit*.

Grit means taking on challenges one day at a time. Minute after minute, hour after hour, day after day.

You can build up grit by keeping in mind that we only have to survive from one moment to the next!

Do the right thing at this very moment, even when no one is watching.

13. How Do You Build Grit?

It is virtually the same as tackling a challenge:

1. Ask relevant questions.
2. Answer them honestly.
3. Develop your goals.
4. Carve your goals into realistic, small action steps.
5. Tackle them, one at a time, daily.

Long-term, consistent progress beats short fireworks of efforts every time.

Achieve small successes. Then build momentum from there, one by one, until you get where you want to be.

Consistent baby steps work.

What seems to be happening at snail speed, while we are in the process, in hindsight a year later, amounts to a massive change in a short period of time!

Look back on what you have already achieved! Write down all your successes and accomplishments. Celebrate and reward your wins!

Otherwise, you might run into burnout and demotivation.

Pause for appreciation and literally give yourself a pat on the shoulder.

Then approach the next challenge with a zest for life with the curiosity needed to move and grow through your experiences and challenges.

Know with certainty that you will get there, step by step, by keeping the following eight key areas in life in mind and recalibrating them on an ongoing basis.

This is a compass that serves you for a lifetime.

When habits, routines, and subconscious patterns get the better of you, and they will, it is time to revisit each chapter in this book.

Redirect your-self consciously toward your best possible outcome again and again, steering your ship around cliffs, and into the direction you want it to be in!

The moment you let go of the wheel, the ship goes off course.

Don't blame it on the ship; take control and the wheel back into your own hands! Part II explains how in detail.

PART II

How to Engineer Your Best Possible Outcome

Awareness, action, focus, commitment, consistency, as well as inputs from professionals in their respective fields who are up to date with the latest standards and regulations are all necessary to level up in our lives.

Always look for facts, figures, and information *at the source* to make decisions.

Results can be achieved within months if we give it our full attention, commitment, time, energy, resources, and dedication.

Let's get started!

The Eight Key Areas of Life

1. Health - Energy Is The New Currency

"Health is Wealth."
–Chinese Proverb

Your body is the one thing that stays with you for a lifetime from the cradle to the grave! It is your irreplaceable vehicle through life.

Take great care of it!

Your body is your best friend in innumerable ways.

It can sense what your logic cannot. Trust your gut instinct. If something feels off, it usually is, be it people or circumstances.

Your body sends you the signals when things are not right. Listen to them and take them seriously.

Your mind cannot function without a balanced food intake, proper hydration, exercise, sufficient sleep, and rest time, spending time in nature, and having personal human connections and interactions.

Feeling down or out of it might be an immediate effect of lack in any of these points.

We need to ask ourselves if all these areas are adequately covered and if not, we can remedy them quite quickly before bigger health issues arise. Again, awareness is key. Because of our hectic lifestyle, it has become very fashionable not to sleep enough and to neglect our primary needs.

We might feel depressed when it is our body that does not have enough sleep, or hydration with water, electrolytes (we can buy them inexpensively at any pharmacy), and nutrition with the right vitamins and minerals. Our body is made of around 60 percent water, and for babies, over 70 percent!

If we are dehydrated, our mind will not work well: we will feel disoriented, tired, down, dizzy, heavy, and sleepy, have heart palpitations, no motivation or focus. Take these symptoms very seriously!

Dehydration happens fast.

Being aware of it is essential for our well-being and productivity, especially in climates where we are in air-conditioned or heated rooms and when we exercise. Drinking water does not always work since it sometimes does not contain enough minerals.

That means we can dehydrate even when we drink water!

In this case, take electrolytes in any form. These work almost instantly and can help you quickly recover.

Skip the sugary, high-calorie soda, juices, or smoothies, and coffee, tea, or alcohol.

What the body truly needs is clean, still, room-temperature water.

Health Issues

Some people have food intolerances and allergies and need to watch what they eat. Other people have other health conditions, such as hormonal imbalances, that greatly impact their quality of life.

Certain conditions might as well be caused or aggravated by additives, colorants, preservatives, toxins, pesticides, hormones, antibiotics, and other agents present in processed foods.

Be very careful about what you shop. Read the labels, watch out and educate yourself about what it is that you eat and drink!

The human body is *not* designed to cope with much of what is present nowadays in processed food.

The same goes for hygiene and cosmetic products as well as environmental pollution.

If you face a medical issue, please never give up.

You can often improve your situation and the way that you feel through medications, supplements, Western medicine, Ayurveda medicine, Traditional Chinese Medicine, and more.

Sometimes, the unconventional is what helps. Every person is different and must find the solutions that do work for them. It is your health and your body; no one else lives in it but you. Take it seriously and do not just blindly follow advice.

You have the power to stay healthy and fit by creating a daily rhythm when you eat, sleep, and exercise. Set your alarm to wake up for meals and sleep times as a daily reminder to create new habits as when under stress, we tend to forget and neglect these. Do not ignore your body!

Uneasiness, pain, headaches, swelling, nausea, and sudden weight changes are all warning signs!

Listen to your body. It is your best friend, signaling when things are off.

Your remedy could be as simple as drinking more water, eating healthier, and getting back into a routine with enough movement outside, exercise, social interaction, sunshine, and enough rest.

Improve your environment, too!

Heart palpitations and headaches at night might not necessarily be from anxiety or stress, but something as mundane as a gas pipe leak in your air conditioner or heater!

Check all possible options by excluding what has been proven not to be the cause to find an answer.

Accountability Partner

You know what you need to do. But what if you lack the discipline or awareness to do the right thing? Find an accountability partner!

Someone who can support you to accomplish your goals irrespective of your 'motivation.'

You are not a robot. No one can act in the right manner all the time! Enroll your friend in helping you achieve the best possible outcome.

Do not forget that you need to be your own best friend, too!

Base actions on decisions, not on motivation.

Use your favorite electronic device or app to measure your steps, heart rate, sleep, hydration, and more to measure tangible progress.

With so many options available, it truly IS self-sabotage if you are not taking care of yourself.

Self-sabotage can originate in low self-love, esteem, appreciation and confidence. We will tackle these issues in the following chapters.

Your health is, first and foremost, your responsibility.

Learn what lifestyle works for *you*! Start with small tasks, create winning, healthy experiences for yourself, and then build from there.

You are the only person living with yourself every day for life!

Be your greatest asset. Take care of yourself and become your own best friend!

"All know the way; few actually walk it." –Bodhidharma

For tech enthusiasts, we have health apps and health rings available, giving us specific and bespoke advice on how to improve our readings over time.

Health - Questions to Ask

1. Do I breathe properly? There are different ways to breathe. Learn what they are, their effects, and when to use them.

2. Am I healthy? When am I due for my next medical check-up? What were the results of my last physical? How do I remedy what is wrong? Ask an endocrinologist to get a thorough check-up done.
3. How do I increase my physical **well-being**? Am I doing it? If not, why not? How do I start with small steps?
4. Do I **sleep** enough? Different people need different amounts of sleep; how much sleep do I need to feel rested, happy, and balanced? Every night, ideally, I sleep for x hours. Do I ban electronic devices and work from my bedroom? How can I create a beneficial and soothing evening routine?
5. Do I **exercise?** Do I exercise the way I'd like to be doing it? There is no point in hitting the gym if you hate it. Find an activity that you truly enjoy and look forward to doing. That makes it sustainable and enjoyable.
6. Is my **diet** balanced and healthy? Listen to your body, it usually knows what is best if you really listen. Cut sugar, fried, artificial, and processed foods out of your diet. Eat naturally, in balanced amounts. Extremes are not healthy, they lead to negative physical symptoms. Strive to eat healthy, and your body and long-term well-being will thank you for it!
7. Do I have **food intolerances or food allergies**? This is very important. If you naturally avoid certain foods or feel bad after eating them, you might have a food allergy or intolerance. Get tested by a qualified medical practitioner to learn what you should avoid.
8. What foods do I have to **avoid** out of experience to feel good? Do I do it? If not, why? And how can I start?
9. Do I drink **enough still water** at room temperature? Water is what we are made of. How can I avoid dehydration? Cold drinks are not healthy for our bodies, especially if we have asthma, a cold, or pain.

10. Do I stretch daily to keep my body **flexible,** regardless of my age? T*en minutes* of exercise a day is enough to keep moving easily.
11. Do I enjoy **physical** connection? How comfortable am I with my body, and with giving and receiving pleasure?
12. Do I carry myself with good **posture** and body awareness? Without trained muscles, there is no good posture. Our muscles should support our bone structure, and not just hang from it! What are posture-improving activities that I like and can do?
13. Do I have enough **rest** and get enough **breaks** during the day? Each week? Month? Year? Working without taking breaks is highly inefficient and unhealthy.
14. Do I **dress** in a way that shows that I value myself and reflects who I am or who I want to be? First impressions *do* count, no matter what style you like.
15. Do I have a head-to-toe **hygiene** routine? Pay special attention to your feet and your toes. They are the *foundation* on which you stand every day of your life! Do keep them clean and healthy.
16. Are my actions and **behavior** beneficial to my health, or are they damaging my body and me? Change and get help from an expert or therapist if necessary.

2. Mindset - The Inner Operating System

"If you correct your mind, the rest of your life will fall into place."
–Lao Tzu

One of the most important skills in life is to master our own mindset and our self-communication. Your attitude is formed by your thoughts, the meaning you attach to them, and how you act on them. How you communicate with yourself determines your circumstances and life events!

> You regularly update your electronic devices.
> When was the last time you upgraded your own mind-set?

Did you get rid of outdated thoughts and belief systems that do not serve you any longer?

Think about your thoughts.

> What thoughts are swirling around in your head every day? Are you aware of them?

> Where and which year are they from? Who put some of them there?

> How old were you when it happened?

If these are negative thoughts, they can inhibit your life force and energy substantially and affect your health, especially in times of uncertainty and worry.

In many Asian countries, they call untrained thoughts the "monkey mind."

If your thoughts are constantly jumping around, you are prone to feeling worried, distracted, unproductive, and often miserable.

Overthinking leads to a lack of focus on what is important in the here and now.

Successful people make decisions quickly and act on them.

Why is it so important to get a grip on your thought process?

"Whatever you hold in your mind on a consistent basis is exactly what you will experience in your life." –Anthony Robbins

Life is way too short to be where we do not want to be, with thoughts and people we do not want to spend our life energy on or with! Stop it.

How Not to Listen to the Little Voice in Your Head

If we pay attention to the little voice in our head, we might become aware that it is most often hostile, belittling, and even insulting (depending on what we hear growing up), which is highly detrimental to reaching our goals and ambitions.

With a bad "friend" like this, we are ridden with anxiety and lose courage before we even get started! So, let's look at how to quiet it down.

Often the little voice's whole aim is to keep us safe. Whatever you have done in our life so far has been successful, and you have survived (otherwise, you wouldn't be reading or listening to this right now).

Why is this inner voice so persistent? Any change or new input is first and foremost, considered a threat to the status quo. Your body has a built-in danger response to trying new and unfamiliar things. The unfamiliar often used to mean danger, exclusion, and often, certain untimely death. The human brain has not evolved fast enough to catch up with the latest technology and modern society. It does not realize that today, doing new and unfamiliar things is rarely a death threat, as it was hundreds and thousands of years ago when we were excluded from the group, and left alone to fight or die.

The good news is that you can help your brain catch up to the 21st century!

We can overcome the power of the little voice by becoming aware of our own thoughts.

This visualization I first heard from Blair Singer helps:

Imagine the little voice as a little buddy who is sitting on your shoulder, trying to call your attention to avoid change at all costs.

Imagine to duct tape its mouth (it is a visual, not a reality) and tap him reassuringly on the shoulder. Tell him that it will all be okay and proceed to take action regardless!

The more we practice soothing it, the more we gain mastery over the little voice in our head.

The Power of the Mind

"Do not be pushed by your problems. Be led by your dreams!"

Try this: *Do NOT* think about a green elephant with a red tail!

Now, what are you instantly thinking about? A green elephant with a red tail!

Even though I said "do not," think about it.

The same goes for "I don't want to…

> become overweight
> fail my exams, be broke, be
> miserable, etc.
> It creates the opposite of what you want!

We do attract the very things we do not want because our brain is incapable of processing negation and follows what we focus on.

Instead, focus on what you do want and state it in the present tense.

Let's flip our list above:

> I am slim and healthy,
> I succeed in my exams,
> I have abundance in my life,
> I am happy and fulfilled.

This feels a lot better, doesn't it? How about:

"I am happy, healthy, wealthy, prosperous, fulfilled, safe, and successful."

Does it scare you? How does it feel to say this sentence out loud every day in the morning?

Your mind will start to focus on the opportunities that will get you there!

Followed up by taking action and learning daily; this will change the course of your life over time in a whole different direction!

This is one of THE key factors to success! Big-picture thinking plus emotional integration can help you gain great resilience in achieving your goals consistently.

You will have found that anger, fear, disappointment, anxiety, and your own brew of inner turmoil will not be constructive states to be in to reach them.

"Holding on to anger is like holding a hot coal with the intent of throwing it at someone else; we are the one who get burnt." –Buddha

Every Day, Write Your Goals Down on Paper!

Remember, one great technique that *does* work is writing your goals down on paper every day. This takes just 5 minutes.

Focusing on your goals without censoring them in your mind will lead you toward achieving them. Writing pulls your thoughts from abstraction into physical reality and helps you to anchor them in your mind and body.

You don't need to show your paper to anyone. Keep it safe and carry it with you as a compass to guide your decisions throughout the day.

It will help you assess if an action leads you away from (contraction) or towards (expansion) your goals.

Whenever you feel doubtful, insecure, or lost, focus your vision and mind on your inner compass and if something feels contracting or expanding to you.

Ask for What You Want

"Ask for what you want and be prepared to get it." –Maya Angelou

Reset the compass of your self-communication; it will change your life!

You will literally rewire your brain.

One of my mentors I had over the years instructed me to say to myself daily in the morning:

"No matter what, something good comes out of everything!" and

"Something fantastic is going to happen to me today!" Give it a go. Most of the time, it does!

"We become what we think." –Buddha

If you think negatively about yourself or that you cannot do something, you are reinforcing that belief and outcome!

Yet whatever negatives you are thinking about are not the whole story.

Recall your successes and rewire your brain through practice and awareness to create kinder thoughts of and for yourself, and for others, daily.

We react to others as *we perceive ourselves*, the way we see the world, and our opinions about how things in life are supposedly meant to be.

Hence, we are heavily biased and limited in our perceptions.

We need not just friends, they are usually too similar to us as we tend to seek out people who have aligned likes and dislikes as friends. Seek neutral mentors to help you see the world and situations through a completely different lens than just your own, and receive inputs based on a different set of experience, knowledge, and background.

Choose wisely whom you let into your head space!

Ask others for information, inputs, support, connections, and help when and where required.

There is a 50: 50 chance you will get it, and if not, you will still be in the same position as you were in before asking. Nothing to lose, everything to win!

"Ask, and you shall be given."

How to Create a Better Version of Yourself Step-by-Step

1. Create the best version of yourself by stating in detail who you want to become.
2. Write your goals down every day.

3. Ask for what you want.

When you say: "I am," whatever follows it is likely to come true! Make sure it is a great statement!

Consistent, positive reinforcement will create a profound change in not just how you see yourself but how others perceive you.

Life is not about finding yourself but about creating yourself!

We are treated the way we see and carry ourselves, and according to what we tolerate.

Setting and enforcing boundaries is crucial to maintaining our own well-being and safety.

On this note, here is a very important warning:

If abuse is involved in interaction with others, be it psychological, mental, physical, sexual, time-wise, spiritual, emotional, financial, space-wise, or in relation to what you own, DO ENFORCE strict boundaries, if necessary, by force of the law. Make sure you are safe.

One clear NO is a full sentence, and if disrespected enough, do take appropriate measures to protect yourself.

It is the other person's issue of not being able to deal with limitations and their own challenges in an appropriate manner.

You are not responsible to re-educate or save grown adults as third parties unless it is written in your job description.

Get yourself to a safe and peaceful place without them.

If this seems impossible, *you* need professional help and support to get out of such highly toxic relationships and behavioral patterns.

Be aware that if you grew up in an abusive environment, it takes a lot of inner work and healing with a professional therapist to be able to recognize red flags early. Others from functional homes would run for the hills from the get-go and avoid toxic people altogether upon first telltale signs!

When everything feels too much, believe that.

Focus on one breath, one moment at a time, and give the rest up to higher power.

You lead the way, I do the work, it is a great way to cope with change.

It requires trust in something bigger than yourself.

It will all work out if you keep going and don't give up! One more step at a time is all it takes.

How to Break Bad Thinking Habits

Anytime you discover which thoughts belittle, ridicule, diminish you and keep you trapped, you might want to write them down and then consider:

- Where do these thoughts come from?
- Which people did you adopt them from growing up?

— Are you taking over the negative voices of parents, family, friends, teachers, bullies, or other people who had an influence on you in your childhood or teenage years?

After you learn about having these negative thoughts, how can you stop thinking about them?

To break a bad mind habit, such as thinking endlessly about missed opportunities or repeating denigrating thoughts, try this simple method, which you might have heard about:

Wear a rubber band around your wrist. Snap it each time you realize you are having a negative thought or using a negative word against yourself.

Let me explain why this can help to break the pattern. Human beings prefer pleasure over pain. Our brain naturally wants to avoid the snap of pain. Gradually, it will shy away from the behavior that causes the pain.

Give your brain time to catch on, become fully aware and change negative patterns.

Reconditioning yourself to kinder thoughts and behavior is a process.

The efforts will be rewarded.

You'll gain greater control of own life and thinking patterns by developing the ability to actively change them.

Improving your life starts literally inside out!

Acquire Mindfulness

"Knowing others is intelligence; knowing yourself is true wisdom." –Lao Tzu

How do I **communicate** with myself in my head?

1. How **aware** and **mindful** am I from 1 - 10? Do I keep **learning** every day? How can I move the number a bit higher today?
2. Do I know how to **calm down** my mind? Do I know how to **be present** in the moment? The breathing exercise is a great help!
3. Do I know what **I want**? Do I **act** on it? How **honest** am I with myself?
   "You cannot know your real mind as long as you deceive yourself." –Bodhidharma
4. How do I deal with praise and criticism or **rejection**?
   "As solid rocks remain unmoved by the wind, so the wise remain unmoved by blame and praise." –Buddha
5. Do I know how to set **intentions** on what I want? In the beginning was the word; before the word was the thought. **We can create** our own thoughts!
6. Am I aware of the power of my **thoughts**? What helps me to **unclutter** my mind?
7. How do I deal with **fear**? Are there better ways?
8. Do I know how to **let go**?
9. Do I know how to **forgive**?
   Do I know how to truly **move on**?
10. Do I know how to **focus** on my vision, mission, and goals?
    "Where there is a will, there is a way." –Proverb
11. Do I know how to manage **stress** and **uncertainty**?

12. Do I understand the importance of **silence**?
    "Silence is the source of great strength." –Lao Tzu
13. Do I know how to manage my **time** and **expectations**?
    "Expect much from yourself and little from others, and you will avoid incurring resentment." –Confucius
14. Do I know how to be in **flow** when what I say, feel, and do are aligned?
15. What am I truly **passionate** about?
16. How do I know what is **true** for me?
17. What is **my WHY**?
18. How do I want to live for the rest of my life starting today, here, and now?

3. EQ - The Invisible Advantage

Your emotions, identity, family history, roots, and relationships are topics that relate to a level of existence called soul.

I like to state that the specific weight of the soul is not given; it must be earned.

We can't borrow, buy, lend, fake, or take it.

The soul is not the body, when your soul is tired, sleep won't help.

Once you gain more clarity in how to identify and deal with your emotions, life becomes a much more pleasant journey.

You are not strapped helplessly to a rollercoaster anymore.

You gain the freedom to choose your actions, gain more insights, and have more self-awareness and self-control. Let's explore this further.

Emotions: Are They Yours or Are You Theirs?

We **have** emotions. But we **are not** our emotions.

This insight enables you to learn how to deal with all sorts of overwhelming negative feelings, such as frustration, anger, disappointment, jealousy, and again, *fear*. Humans are naturally fear-driven, hence why it is so hard to consciously change direction.

When you feel overwhelmed with negative emotions, you will become the victim of your own inner turmoil.

To regain control, you will first need to calm down!

This is an excellent time to use the breathing exercise.

The three-minute breathing exercise gives you a way to distance yourself both mentally and physically from the destructive intensity of your negative feelings.

Acknowledge Your Feelings

Even though your feelings are not yours, it is important to give them healthy respect.

Learn to love yourself *before* you judge your feelings, or decide they need to be changed.

Honor, respect, and acknowledge your needs, and your feelings.

Take them seriously!

They are just as valid as anyone else's and a passport to your inner freedom!

Listen to and acknowledge (but not necessarily act on) them, for two reasons:

They can teach you a lot about yourself.
They can teach you a lot about what you want.
They teach you about what is currently not right in your life.

Use them to help you focus on making the necessary changes to attain what makes you more fulfilled.

No one else can tell you how you feel or feel your feelings for you!

Explore Your Identity

Your roots must be deep and strong to withstand the storms and challenges that life throws at you.

Going deeper allows you to know who you are below the surface and anchor yourself in meaning that will make you a lot stronger.

Your identity is part of intergenerational family history and part of your personal background, which includes your family of origin, upbringing and the unique experiences and choices you made that make you: you!

If you are not aware of who you are and what you are made of, at your core, you will not be able to choose a direction in life that you will like, and that makes you unique, no matter how hard you try.

Instead, you will be repeating the same patterns that run in your family, regardless of whether you like or detest them. If unchecked, this will go on for generations without family members even realizing it.

That is why it is so important to gain as much knowledge as possible about your history, ancestry, roots, the history of your family, and their life stories. We can't change what we don't know and are not aware of, become able to *break the cycle,* and make conscious choices in our own lives without doing this work.

Otherwise, you might feel the push and urge to act in a certain way without really wanting to and without understanding why you are doing it.

Your DNA has evolved from all those who came before you!

We are all connected, and our stories are passed on genetically to us, becoming our story! This is how humans evolved for generations.

Talk to your elders. Ask them about the stories of your family members, whatever they can tell you, up to two generations back or even more if possible. Understand your core makeup.

This consists of the story of your parents and your grandparents, who are the people closest to you, on a DNA level, and all about who you are. The older you get, the more you will recognize their stories weaving through your own life.

The more you know, it will become easier to decide whether you want to make similar choices as they did or go a *different* (not opposing) path.

If you do not know about them, you will not get the chance to consciously decide for yourself.

Strive to know who they were, what kinds of choices they made, and how they ended up. This is the true legacy of their existence, which they have left to you, and that goes far beyond an inheritance, intentions, or material wealth.

How to Arrange Your Family Tree

You are, on the top of your ancestral pyramid:

You (and siblings)

Mother (M)   Father (F)

Grandmother (M)-Grandfather (M) Grandmother (F) –
Grandfather (F) Great-grandmother (M) Great-grandfather
(M) Great-grandfather (F) Great-Grandmother (F)
G-G-grandmother (M) G-G-grandfather (M) G-G- grandfa-
ther (F) G-G-Grandmother (F)

Further add in the siblings that each of your parents and grandparents had in order of their birthdate from left (oldest) to right (youngest), and it will give a detailed overview of your family background and ancestry. Learn more about this systemic approach if you are interested in getting to the root of things by reading the book "*It Didn't Start With You.*"

Even if you never had the chance to meet certain members of your family, they *still* influence you in profound ways simply through their existence in your family tree, resonating with you on a subconscious level. How is this possible? Imagine a family system visually as if it is like a nursery mobile hanging over a baby's cot. If you pull an element out of position, the entire mobile gets affected.

If you look into your family members' history, you will start to recognize characteristics and events that run deep within your family structure. These can be likes and dislikes, tendencies and quirks, and certain behaviors or movements that are not just yours. You are recognizing life events that have happened *before*, and fates that seem to repeat themselves. Similar traits can skip one generation, and grandchildren often display traits of their grandparents!

You are the product of a family that made many decisions prior to your birth.

None of them were your choice.

We are a combination of nature and nurture.

Yet how you decide to change the course of your own life, this decision and making it a reality going forward is your very own choice!

It is a process, and not easy to live the life you really want and to end negative family cycles.

The first step is becoming aware of the patterns.

This will allow you to work on consciously breaking the chain of repetition. This is often hard and painful, but necessary to overcome the past.

Once you know where an issue that you experience develops, you can then start to heal.

Often, you will realize that something you blamed yourself for is an issue that did not start with you!

The same is true of your expectations. We often identify needs such as career and life choices as our own, when they were passed on to us from previous generations.

Out of love, we fulfill our parents' unlived dreams, and unfulfilled aspirations. Set yourself free to pursue your path.

Further, we often do not know why we do not feel fulfilled in our lives, although we have seemingly attained all the external hallmarks of success, money, career, belongings, health, relationships, status.

However, the personal unfulfillment remains.

When there is emptiness inside, it keeps you up at night. It leads you into the same midlife crisis your parent or grandparent had, as you are thinking the same thought they once did: *there must be more to life than this.*

But with this awareness, my goal for you is to be able to define and choose your identity based on knowledge. Not based on living in pure opposition to, or unconsciously following, representing or taking over someone else's history.

None of these allow you free choice to live your life path.

Get Your Skeletons Out of the Closet

We all face traumatic experiences, and we try to avoid their memories under all circumstances. Yet, what we resist persists…

And with the next trigger, we experience full-on flashback experiences.

Not only does unprocessed trauma remain in the body, but it blocks our ability as well to choose the life we want to live. We cannot have a free choice without knowing and accepting what happened and what IS and disconnecting the emotional response from the possible triggers.

Know that before you start to feel better, you might feel worse.

Get your family's and your own skeletons out of the closet. Give it a thorough spring cleaning!

There will be hurdles to overcome and jammed doors to open.

Secrets are secrets for a reason, they are wrapped in thick layers of perceived guilt and shame.

Yet like cancer does not get treated by putting on a band-aid, neither do secrets and trauma cease to have a toxic influence on us by trying to ignore, deny, or suppress them. Truth hurts greatly.

Just like in surgery cutting out the diseased tissue, it is a powerful agent for real change and eventual healing and acceptance.

We have the choice of living a glossed-over version of our life or becoming fully authentic and stepping into our true power.

Once the dust settles, your vision gets a lot clearer (sometimes literally).

You can fully heal and move in the direction that you really want to go.

The only way to change a human being is to see and accept them for who they truly are and let them reveal their true colors. Accept what you see to notice the truth. Pay attention to what IS, not what you would like to be true.

Do not start to rationalize, excuse, or tolerate things that are clearly not aligned with your values. Then make your decision. Accepting does not mean staying. You do have a choice.

"Tension is who we think we should be. Relaxation is who we are." –Chinese Proverb

Act

Especially in our younger years, we usually know what we do *not* want, and struggle heavily to figure out what we *do* want due to our upbringing, constantly being told what to do by family, school, peers, and society.

We struggle to choose career, car, spouse, house, family, and lifestyle, all the way down to what to do on the week end, where to eat for dinner, and what kind of activities to do before bed.

We all know people who are highly habit-driven, do not like to think for themselves, are without awareness or reflection, nor display a desire for either of them, often choosing to numb out and compensate for their pain instead of head-on dealing with it.

The struggle to choose our path is very real, and it can be observed everywhere. We are not encouraged to break out of any given system.

Yet if you do want to create a life on your terms, there is no way around it.

"It is your life, but only if you make it so." —Eleanor Roosevelt

Worry takes your energy, motivation, and time, and leaves you stuck in a bad situation. Consider this: If you have time to worry, you do have time to take focused action instead!

Dare and move forward, put yourself in charge, and allow yourself to thrive! Yes, it takes effort, courage, discipline, work, vision, and determination. The very things that true leaders are made of.

Become the captain of your own ship!

Consider this: In real life-or-death situations, there is no time for worry! The shock of it jolts you into taking massive action for survival. Logic is too slow. There is no time to ponder. Your survival instinct kicks in, and it is seldom wrong. Listen to it.

Trust in life and yourself to be able to make the necessary changes and adjustments when and where necessary.

You will have to as life continuously changes around every seven to ten years. Leap forward!

Grow Grit

Grit is the ability to persevere, overcome, and move forward despite challenges, failures, and obstacles. When giving up or failure is not an option, you prime yourself to give your very best.

Because you want to survive or win, there is no plan B.

When you genuinely need a successful outcome, you add an intensity to it that does not let you quit, no matter what.

Notice that when you look at the life stories of highly successful people, they rarely had it easy.

On the contrary, they often have faced enormous hardships and trauma and made great sacrifices to achieve their goals that often seemed impossible.

It is impossible until it is done, as the saying goes.

Ask yourself:

– What is it that I can do now to improve the situation I am worrying about?
– How can I improve who I am right now?

Make it measurable and specific. Define what you will improve and by when. Then, put in the hard work.

Laser focus on the outcome you want to achieve, and "the how" will fall into place.

Remember, your brain will create in real life whatever you focus on. So put *all* of your attention on what you *do want*. This reinforces the creation of your best possible outcome!

Solutions exist that you do not even know about yet. You WILL find them… not by overthinking but by taking action, again, and again towards your goals. Daily. Step by step. Breathe. Keep going, and doors will open.

Your worry will subside and be replaced by results.

Grit means patience and perseverance. They are key.

Life will test you if you truly want something. Do not give up on yourself.

"Without dreams of hope and pride, a man will die. Though his flesh still moves, his heart sleeps in the grave." –C. Mangione

You Only Can Love Someone Else…If You Love Yourself

"Mastering others is strength. Mastering yourself is true power." –Lao Tzu

If we do not love ourselves, we will not allow anyone else to love us.

Without self-love, we will not feel worthy and deserving. *"Love your neighbor as yourself"* –Torah

In fact, we will sabotage our lives, destroying the good things we have, often without even realizing that we are doing it.

Why is this?

Our beliefs shape our self-perception. This includes how we treat ourselves and hence, other people. Low self-esteem and self-hatred often come from a place of confusion, guilt, shame, and feeling lost.

Love, kindness, forgiveness, grace, patience, understanding, good communication, loyalty, care.

We cannot give, what we have not experienced ourselves and what we do not know!

There is anger and sadness in being cut off from our roots.

I think that is why the Sankofa in Ghana have a saying: "A people without knowledge of its history, origin, and culture is like a tree without roots."

In our society, the connection to our roots is often so tenuous and deemphasized that most people are not in the least aware of the powerful effect this has on them.

Without knowing who you truly are, there will always be a hole in your core being, nagging away at your happiness.

Your family members are like the branches of a tree. Each grows in a different direction. On the surface, they do not have to look the same. However, they grow from the same roots, which are buried and hidden yet planted deep into the ground.

This root connection in our families cannot be changed, no matter how much we want it to be different.

Think about it, the roots are the nourishment of the tree. Learn how to be fed by your roots. Reconnect to your source.

This does not mean you have to physically meet family members who harmed you. What it means is to learn what was and what is in its details, do the inner work, and accept life for what it was and what it is.

It means to give yourself the gift of making peace through genuine acceptance.

This will set you free to focus your inner resources and energy forward to consciously building the new, and not out of opposition or subconscious pattern repetition.

Once aware, learn to integrate the parts of your past that are dragging you down to rob them of their power over you. It is what it is.

There are parts that are not essentially you; make a conscious choice to release them back into the past now that you understand where they came from.

"Let go of anger. Let go of pride. When we are bound by nothing, we go beyond sorrow." –Buddha

Being conscious, aware, grateful, and respectful of your ancestors, no matter what happened in previous generations, accepting that we are imperfect humans, will allow you to fully accept the flow of life from your roots coming through to you.

You can then receive their blessings and step into the responsibility of making the best out of your own life now.

To honor your ancestors who came before you over so many generations, their lifetimes, their efforts, their suffering and joys, their stories, and their fates.

Without them, you would not exist today.

Letting go with gratitude and love for yourself and others releases you from the prison of resentment, hurt, bitterness, and pain.

This jail is built by blaming the past and its people. We isolate ourselves from our life force and stay put, refusing to grow.

Drop the weight of what you cannot change.

We are not going to alter someone else's fate by suffering for them nor carrying their burden or identifying with it; the burdens of our ancestors are theirs, yet they remain our roots where they came from.

Know that everything in our life can be distilled into just a few words: "Thank you for giving me life. Thank you for this lesson.

It is up to me to make the best out of it now." Transcend your pain through gratitude.

"We come to love not by finding a perfect person, but by learning to see a person perfectly." –Sam Keen

The better we know, acknowledge, accept, love, and take care of ourselves, the better we can do the same for others.

Love is all about giving without expectations, need, or righteousness.

It comes from a place of sharing, humility, loyalty, compromise, and service. Even if, at times it is safer to love from a distance, true love doesn't know space or time. It just IS.

Be enough to yourself and be comfortable with your own company. Become able to be alone. Become the person you want to be with.

Then, you can be an equal partner for someone else and display the positive traits that you crave in another person.

Give yourself first what you crave from others!

Being whole and self-reliant enables you to build a relationship based on mutual respect, sharing, and loving interaction between two fully functional and accountable adults.

You might as well notice that your attraction patterns will change away from subconscious instant trauma recognition in another person, for which the butterflies in your stomach are a surefire sign of.

The nervous system recognizes the danger of re-enacting the old drama!

Once you have done your work, you will become able to create stable, reliable, and healthy relationships.

For a trauma-addicted person this seems boring and not at all appealing or interesting. Stay away.

Striving to come from a place of wholeness and fulfillment will give you more power over creating the outcomes that you want to achieve in life.

Neediness and unrealistic expectations carry unresolved trauma, confusion, and codependency to a certain degree.

You operate like a puppet pulled by the strings of you, and your family's triggers and past.

We are all here to learn.

A healthy relationship has the ability and strength to hold the space for each other's vulnerability, trauma, memories, and growth without enmeshment.

Come with a filled plate, able to share your meal.

If you are both starving and longing to be fed, what you have got is a recipe for disaster.

Your relationship will be mired in blame, conflict, frustration, helplessness, emotional rollercoasters, arguments, and outbursts of misdirected and confused anger.

The same happens if only one person in the relation ship is making efforts, while the other one is only taking. Co-dependency is far from a healthy relationship dynamic.

It needs two grown and mature individuals who are doing the work to provide for each other a safe space to live and grow in, apart and together.

They both need to have adequate communication and conflict resolution skills, self-awareness, respect, and honesty to be able to enforce healthy boundaries and thrive as a couple.

You want loved ones to be able to trust that you can take responsibility for your well-being and emotions. That you are reliable yet capable of vulnerability, sharing your struggles and failures, and seeking help where and when it is required.

Having a partner, especially a life partner, requires work and trust.

You and your feelings must be safe, with your partner and their feelings, and they must be and feel safe with you. So, you can bond in love, intimacy, and mutual respect.

This will allow both of you to make healthy choices and create a fulfilling relationship and a fulfilling life together in mutual agreement, respect, and consent.

"Being deeply loved by someone gives you strength, while loving someone deeply gives you courage."
–Lao Tzu

How to Change from Negative to More Balanced Emotions

We have already learned that our brains are hard-wired to remember, and often repeat, negative things.

This is what keeps us from uncertainty and danger.

However, this also predisposes us to attract more negativity into our lives as they seem familiar and hence predictable.

How can we change this dynamic?

Make a CONSCIOUS daily effort to choose and to remember **the good**: your successes as well as the nice and happy memories of your day, past, and your family. This is where mind-discipline and gratefulness come into play.

Recall that we were born, and we have survived everything until now. We are champions of survival. Start leaving a legacy of positive thinking.

A legacy that goes beyond just remembering the bad, suffering and resentment.

Elevate yourself to a place where life is worth living. And to an attitude worth remembering.

"Let your own light shine, so that we give others the permission to do the same. Our deepest fear is not that we are inadequate. Our deepest fear is that we are powerful beyond measure."
– Marianne Williamson

Forgiveness and Gratitude

Happiness comes with gratefulness in your heart; it is in equal measure to how grateful you are.

Until you forgive, you will not be able to feel grateful, which is the key to joy.

Most religious texts teach us to honor our parents for this very reason. We do not honor them for what they have done or who they have been, but simply because they brought us into this existence.

We honor our parents because they gave us life.

If you can honor your parents, and the fact that they gave you your life, you will be able to accept your life and its blessings fully.

Why have you been hurt by people you love, and even people who love you? Hurt people usually hurt others, often because they are not aware and do not know any better. We are all capable of it.

"Forgive them, for they do not know what they are doing." —Jesus

"And forgive us our trespasses, as we forgive them the trespasses against us." —Matthew, 6:12-14

Regardless, on the receiving end, it hurts, and forgiveness is often difficult.

It can be especially difficult to forgive our parents or families for the pain that we have felt because of their words and actions, the very people that were supposed to love and protect us growing up.

They were far from perfect, and so are we.

"Those who cannot forgive others break the bridge over which they themselves must pass." —Confucius

We must let go of resentment for our own sake:

What we have experienced in childhood does not have to define our entire lifetime!

Blaming and focusing on others' perceived shortcomings keeps us passive and victimized.

If we decide to let it all go, we free ourselves to live a healthy life in which we can focus on what we can change, ourselves, moving from victim to victor.

If you grew up in a healthy and fully functional family, congratulations, you won the lottery in life!

Forgiving Yourself Is Hard to Do

The hardest person to forgive is yourself.

Guilt, shame, and the turmoil of feeling worthless do not come from being hurt *perse* but from the *isolation and loneliness* you feel after being hurt, keeping the secrets secret.

If you do not have an anchor, if you lack awareness that goes beyond your being, it is very easy to feel lost.

Often, we allow our choices and the events that have happened in our lives to define us, especially when we are told to do so.

However, we have also learned that we are often repeating patterns that run in the system of our family roots.

It is up to us to free ourselves and break out of the secrecy.

You CAN raise yourself above and beyond those who wronged you or your wrongdoings, if you forgive and decide to do and be better.

Forgive, and grant yourself to achieve the life that you deserve. Make your ancestors, going back generations, proud and all their sacrifices worth it.

No one exists within and by themselves.

Acknowledge your roots, be proud of all you achieve and the conscious changes you make, and one day you will be the grandfather or grandmother future generations look back to with awe and admiration if you raise the bar for yourself.

Your conscious actions today can change the course of entire generations to come, and not just for your own lineage.

"Forgiveness is the sign of strength." –Dalai Lama

If you think forgiving is a sign of weakness, you have never tried to do it.

Forgiving someone who wronged you is truly hard!

Forgive others regardless of whether you feel they deserve forgiveness in your eyes. You are not the judge of it and need to understand:

> The point is not that *they* did terrible things.
> **The point is that *you* deserve peace!**

Do whatever you can to free yourself and your health from bitterness, anger, resentment, and hate. Focus on what you can control, yourself.

"If you want a happy life, tie it to a goal. Not to people or things." –Albert Einstein

Forgiveness Leads to Fulfillment

The puzzle pieces of your identity can now start to align, forming the picture of who you are and why. This allows you to consciously choose who you want to become and break the chains of the past.

"Let go of anger. Let go of pride. When you are bound by nothing, you go beyond sorrow." –Buddha

Once you know, you do not have to repeat the fate of your family members.

Now you can change habits adopted without a second thought and operate from a mindset that is not your own.

Your influencers also include your friends and social circles, as well as your colleagues. Study them.

Consider uncluttering your life from negative and unwanted influences.

Eagles do not fly with ducks.

Boundaries - Your Garden, Your Gate

The clearer you know who you are, the easier it will be to choose the people you allow to enter your life, as well as your mind.

Imagine that you are like a well-kept garden. To keep it growing as you intend, you must build a fence around yourself so that not just anyone can enter. No one should be allowed to destroy what you have beautifully arranged and planted. No one should be given access to rip up what you have lovingly cared for and grown over so many years.

Anyone is free to admire your garden by looking over the wall. They are not free to tread across it and ravage your plants!

Keep a gate that you can choose to open and close for those who are worthy and respectful visitors in your garden.

You are the gatekeeper of the garden of your life.

Open the gate whenever you want, but make sure the people are deserving of your choice!

As you can see, boundaries and enforcing them are very important. Children and adults alike naturally look for them, sometimes to extremes to find them and test the rules.

At times, you might make the mistake of letting someone questionable into your garden who drains your energy or uses more resources than you wish to share. This is why knowing yourself is so important. To keep your boundaries intact, you must remain true to yourself.

How can you do this without self-awareness and a
- solid understanding of who you are
- what you like or don't like
- a strong sense of your values and belief system
- strong communication skills
- as well as a thorough understanding of human psychology to be able to read situations and people, and avoid being manipulated and taken advantage of?

We all make mistakes, and the wisdom we carry is based on our life experiences, not books.

Honor your mistakes as the life lessons they are, and you need to grow into the person you are today.

Use tough love and tough action if required to safeguard your space, health, peace, and sanity from those who try to take advantage of it.

There is a place for kindness and for giving. Yet ask yourself before you act or overextend:

Why am I willing to give? Am I trying too hard to be liked, accepted, and wanted? What is my pay off by doing this?

Many people are scrupulous takers without remorse. If this is the case, stop, cut your losses, and move on. If you can't although you want to, please seek qualified help.

A healthy person will never exploit you, or make you beg for their attention.

Don't collect red flags!

When You Fail - We All Do at Times
After you fail, reset your vision to the best possible outcome.

Focus on the solution, not the problem. Take massive action to reach a positive, self-defined outcome.

When you are afraid, you do nothing. Fear keeps you passive. Exploited. Victimized. Procrastinating.

Life shrinks or expands in proportion to your *courage*!

Learn how to do things afraid, and your courage will grow by taking action.

"Become a tour guide in your life and not a tourist." –Dennis Waitley

The issues of your ancestors may have been passed down for generations. You do not have to carry them forward if you do the work:

"It stops here and now with me."

Free your children from this hereditary fear and pain. When you take a stand, and draw a line in the sand, you allow yourself and your children to make choices in life undaunted by the emotional ghosts of the past.

Give them a full blessing for prosperity.

As you gain self-knowledge, gratitude, forgiveness, boundaries, and fulfillment, your relationships will significantly improve, becoming more balanced and enjoyable. Instead of repeating the old patterns, you are now free to create what works for you.

Sparkle and shine. Do not apologize for being you!

It is not only possible to follow your dreams, *but an absolute necessity for fulfillment.*

Those who have abandoned their dreams are like ships without a compass on the sea of life not reaching their destination. They are staying in the safe harbor, floating in the same spot. This is not what ships are built for!

Questions to Ask Your EQ

1. What are my **family roots** and **history**?
2. Do I know each **family member's fate,** back to my grandparents?
3. Am I aware of the **patterns** and **secrets** that run in my family? How am I connected?
4. Am I aware of my **emotions**? How do I deal with my emotions? What is my temperament?
5. How do I rate the quality of my **self-worth, esteem, respect, love,** and **belief** on a scale of 1 to 10?
6. How do I **communicate** with others?
7. Do I observe and **learn** from others?
8. Do I know how to **apologize** and how to **forgive**?
9. Do I know how to **let go**? Am I **accepting** what IS?
10. What am I **grateful** for? Do I give others credit for their **influence** on my life?
11. How do I **want to feel**?
12. How do I **enjoy** my life?
13. How do I deal with **uncertainty**? How do I **persevere**?
14. How do I know **my truth**?
15. How do I choose my **inner peace**?
    "Peace comes from within. Do not seek it from without."
    –Buddha

4. Values - The Compass Within

"Why separate your spiritual life and your practical life?

To an integral being, there is no such distinction." –Lao Tzu

What is our spirit?

Our spirit represents our values and belief systems. Another way of describing these is through our "why" and "how." For example, *why* do you do what you do? This is a deep inner guide that we all cling to for survival. Make it the conscious center of your life so it will influence your relationships and interactions.

Define your mission:

What are the goals you want to achieve that go beyond mere material and physical wants and needs?

We all believe in something. Whether it's religion, values, science, or common sense and intellect.

Despite the differences in where we find our values, many cultures and people strive for similar principles:

> harmony
> security
> order
> respect
> discipline
> and what is required for survival and fulfillment.

Discovering your spirituality is a conscious choice; adopting inherited beliefs and values is not.

You grow up following the norms of your family, environment, and culture, but these are generally not adaptations that you have chosen.

In early adulthood, you choose for real. Who do you choose to become?

If you *do not* answer it, you will wake up one morning with a life devoid of personal identity and meaning.

You cannot just pick anything. While following a framework is crucial for social acceptance, such as the framework provided by going to school or having a job, if you lose your purpose and identity in the process, it is not a sustainable framework.

Learn the what, the how, and especially the *why* that makes sense for you.

Build a belief system that is deeper than what you can see and that helps you navigate each of your decisions. Root yourself in your belief system. It will provide for you when the physical world does not.

Faith of nearly any kind can sustain you throughout life.

It can help you go beyond your limits to work for positive goals and causes that are greater than yourself.

Faith gives you strength in times of uncertainty and helps you remember gratitude in times of certainty.

Kindness, goodness, and humanitarian values such as equality, trust, and tolerance are high moral values.

Make your conscious personal choice something that is worth fighting for by rooting it in your spiritual values. This will help you and those around you to survive when the world is not fair.

"Turning towards what we deeply love saves us." –Rumi

How to Handle Your Ego

If the spiritual part of you is the good side, the ego is your dark side.

It is not that telling them apart is so difficult. It is that when you have gone to the dark side, it is hard to get out.

The first step, once again, is awareness.

Spirituality leads to expansion; ego leads to contraction.

To access your spiritual self, you need to become aware of the ego. How? Here is one clue: If what you are thinking and feeling is complicated, you are in the ego's grip. Ego is contracts, excludes, serves the self, and is self-centered and narrow-minded.

Spirit expands, includes, simplifies, and serves the greater good.

The story you keep telling yourself as to why you can't succeed is holding you back.

After a certain age, most of what you let enter your mind becomes *your choice with what you focus on.*

From music to books to movies and conversations, believing in every value you were raised with whether from society, your home, or your peers being carried forward without reflection is a mark of unawareness .

I'm saying to analyze what you think, value, and believe, so you can make *conscious choices.*

In doing so, you may feel the natural fear of exclusion and repercussion. Don't let that stop you.

Breathe. Focus on an honest answer for yourself to each question you raise.

Remember that, ultimately, your thoughts and your values are yours.

"Death is not the biggest fear we have; our biggest fear is taking the risk to be alive and express what we really are."
–Don Miguel Ruiz

Listen to your intuition and find the "why" that keeps pushing you forward and guides you. Gradually, with experience, you will gain confidence and more understanding of who you really are.

Regularly take time to reflect on your life. See how far you have come and think about what the next steps are to progress further in each life chapter.

Value and Belief Questions

1. What are my **beliefs**? What is my **belief system**?
   "I wonder if we get what we believe when we die?" –Annie
   Stephany
2. How was this influenced by my **upbringing**?
3. How was this influenced by the **society** or **culture** I grew
   up in?
4. How much of it is my **own choice**?
5. What do I know about various value and belief systems
   and **religions?**
6. What do I know about **philosophy**?
7. What do I know about **ethics**?
8. What do I consciously choose to **believe** in?
9. Where do I belong in my **school of thinking**?
10. What do I want my **identity** to be?
11. Who do I choose to **learn from**? Who do I choose as my
    mentors? Who do I allow to **influence** me? This is my
    conscious **decision**!
12. How do I know what is **true for me**?
13. How can I see **themes** in the **seven-year cycles of my
    life**? (7, 14, 21, 28, 35, 42, 49, 56, 63, 70, 77, 84, 91, 98
    etc.)
14. What are the **challenges and goals** of each **decade** of
    my life? (0, 10, 20, 30, 40, 50, 60, 70, 80, 90, 100.) What
    happened in these years, and what were the major life
    changes or shifts?
15. What is my **Why**?
16. How do I want to live my **remaining life**? (Take the aver-
    age life expectancy in your country and subtract your
    age. This is around how much time you have left if every-
    thing goes well.)
17. What keeps my **life motivation** going?

18. In what situations do I feel positively **challenged, growing,** and **alive?**

→ Ways to Handle Uncertainty

Dealing with uncertainty can be hard, especially when you are uncertain about something highly relevant to you.

When it hurts, when you feel anxiety and stress, how do you keep the personal gains that you have made?

How do you stay in control, positive, productive, and pleasant to be around?

Here are four suggestions that might help:

1. Be careful how you fill your mind. Avoid negative thoughts and actions. The more you can hold off swearing and being vulgar, the better. Strive not to lie, be deceitful, petty, vindictive, falsify what someone else said, or destroy another's reputation.

   Ultimately, this negativity will reflect into your own life.

   Strive to increasingly govern your moods and habits that are within your own control. No matter how it feels, your moods are up to you and depend on what you choose to focus on.

   Instead of being victimized by others, act towards achieving your goals. Achieving success is the best revenge . Focus your energy and resources on your best possible outcome and keep moving forward.

2. Set boundaries even when you are uncertain.
    Start with keeping your space clean and tidy. Make your bed. It may seem ridiculous given how much stress you are under, but this is a good habit, and you want to cultivate it. Your self-respect keeps score!

    Avoid filling your life with bad habits, poor company, clutter, and distractions.

    Focus on creating a healthy life step by step. Start small.

    Do you know how much happiness you can handle? Find out!

    Take care of your body and mind, and spend time outside, in nature, and with good, positive people who want to see you happy, healthy, fulfilled, and succeeding.

    If you do not have any of those in your life, it might be high time to work on your self-worth, and self-esteem and find constructive people to spend your time with.

3. Listen to people's communication and notice red flags
    Here is a list of things to strive to avoid in yourself and others:
    * sarcasm
    * mean-spirited irony
    * ridicule
    * belittling
    * gossip
    * backstabbing
    * self-criticism
    * judgments

- justifications
- excuses
- black-and-white thinking
- catastrophizing
- 'should,' 'must,' and 'try'
- emotional reasoning
- assumptions
- comparison
- exaggeration

Once you identify these thinking styles, notice them. Now, no one is perfect and always in control. Yet, being aware of these red flags is important.

Distance yourself from people as much as possible who regularly and deliberately display this kind of behavior. They drain your energy and authority.

This distance will allow you to see a negative situation that you are facing in a more distant and helpful way.

4. Your body responds when you are overwhelmed or in crisis.
   You will feel yourself spinning, exhausted, drained, and unable to focus. Your immune system goes down.

To get yourself out of it, reassess and rebalance with the breathing exercise.

What do you need?

Think about how you ideally want to live and then move toward that direction, with every single decision and step!

Identify the gaps with the earlier mentioned questions framework and start closing them one by one.

Once your mind is cleared of self-doubts and fear, it will move you more efficiently toward your goals with single-minded focus and dedication.

It might take a few weeks, months, or even years of consistent effort, yet eventually, you will get there! Keep your eyes on the vision and your actions relentlessly guided towards your goals. Patience!

It is well worth it!

"Logic can get you from A to B. Imagination will take you everywhere." –Albert Einstein

5. Celebrate your successes and important life events, both the small and the big ones.

    Get over any sense that you "do not deserve" to be happy or celebrate yourself.

    Keep your spirit high by rewarding yourself for the hard work you have done and the results you have achieved!

    Give yourself a big pat on your shoulder!

5. Legacy - The Ripple Effect

"Life's most persistent and urgent question is, 'What are we doing for others?'" –Martin Luther King, Jr.

Your Greater Self is what you are connected to and the impact you want to make outside of yourself.

It begins with questions like:

How do I give back?
What difference do I want to make? What do
I want to be remembered for? What do I
want my legacy to be?

Change Yourself First

So much we read about leadership and success is about what people do to, or for, other people. However, this is not the first step.

The beginning is about what we do for *ourselves*.

What you do…for you! - We can't give from an empty cup.

This is not selfish.

Everything in life is based on duality. We breathe in, and we breathe out, it is a 'give and take.'

Without the balance of the two, we perish, which is why we need self-regulation and self-control to keep healthy and disciplined.

To give to ourselves, and then give to others.

Before being able to take care of others, we need to be able to take care of our own basic needs first.

In fact, this is our very first responsibility as an adult human being.

It is the airplane oxygen-mask principle of "self-first."

Fill your cup with knowledge, resources, time, connections, finances, inner strength, health, happiness, and wisdom.

You will be able to give back in a significant way, which has a lasting impact.

Letting Go

The more we can let go of shiny objects, our attachments, and predefined perspectives, the better we can deal with changing life circumstances. Let go, and dare to jump into the unknown. We must overcome our innate fears of being hurt or losing out.

To succeed, we will first have to bear with the perceived vacuum between letting go and receiving, being empty-handed.

Often, great opportunities come only after we let go of the status quo, what we have and who we are, to become what and who we can be.

Trust and believe in yourself, in life, and in the power of good. Combined with the work you do, you will be on your way to making things happen.

Know that gratification is rarely immediate.

Enduring uncertainty takes courage until the new and desired changes can enter your life.

"Be patient and tough. Someday, this pain will be useful to you." –Ovid

Here is a shortlist to master delayed gratification, frustrations, fears, worries, and insecurities:

1. Do t he breathing exercise daily. Take these 3 minutes for yourself!
2. Physically write down your goals on paper on a daily basis.
3. Focus on, and consistently work towards your best possible outcome, putting in consistent efforts.
4. Exercise, sleep, hydrate , and eat a healthy diet

These are life-changing tools that will create the results that you are looking for.

Success takes *patience*, emotional mastery, and clear inner communication. Focus on what is working and gear your thoughts to desired outcomes.

Take small, daily, consistent actions, step by step.

There is no such thing as overnight success!

Get to Like Yourself

Every minute you dwell on past negative experiences is a lost opportunity to focus on creating your own best possible life moving forward!

Get the right attitude by focusing on *great people.*

It is so important to surround yourself and connect with people who support and believe in you and who will lift you higher.

Great minds discuss matters that move the world forward and make an impact together. You won't hear them gossip or complain.

But what if you do not feel comfortable with other people?

What if you can't feel at ease in your own company, without distractions?

If you can't bear your own company, how do you expect others to bear with you?

Becoming your own best friend creates the foundation and stability that is essential to thrive.

Ignore the naysayers, and avoid negative and destructive people, places, and habits.

Go out there and network to meet new people and build relationships.

If you are an introvert, network remotely online. The world is your oyster!

Interacting with high-caliber people, you will hear a lot less negativity, criticism, gossip, or small talk.

Instead, you will hear more positivity, talking about ideas, projects, value propositions, visions, missions, goals, and ideals. You will hear much more about the present and future possibilities, possible collaborations, and taking deliberate actions toward designing a future you want and like.

This is hard to happen if you do not first work on your awareness, traumas, triggers, shortcomings, communication and conflict-resolution skills, how to read and connect with people authentically, and how to bring value to the table.

Why is this so important?

If we are unaware, our communication partner will be able to play on our emotions and perceptions like on a piano, setting their tune.

If you want to level up, level up first!

Charity - Paying It Forward

There is a relationship between giving and receiving; people who give more tend to get more.

This, however, should not be the motivator.

Charity tends to be a part of personal success and in most scriptures, it is a fixture in the value and belief systems.

Here is how to help others move forward:

Please always ask permission first to assist the person or organization you want to help. What you assume is wanted, might not be.

Like buying and selling, acts of charitable giving are a trans-action of energy, money, time, or goods.

Both the receiver and the giver are important, equal partners.

Without the receiver, there is no giver, and vice versa. So, give respectfully.

Ask what will help. Listen for what is most wanted.

Honoring these boundaries shows respect and is itself a kind of giving.

Be humble and grateful for the privilege to change another person's life, even in small ways.

Giving enhances your energy and balances things in your life. Give without expectations.

This is the tricky part.

Trust that the rewards will show up from the least expected people in other situations, at another point in time. Everything in life contributes to the cycle of give and take, of paying it forward.

Your efforts will come back to you eventually. May it be in the form of chances, opportunities, luck, and fortunate circumstances.

Above all, creating an impact by being of service to others is a deeply satisfying and fulfilling art!

"It is amazing what we can accomplish if we do not care who gets the credit." –Harry S. Truman

You can donate in many ways.
Most think of getting rich first and donating money later.

Why not start small?

There are countless charity organizations happy to take your time, support, and financial donation, as small as it might be.

The fact is, there are many ways to give. If you would like to create an immediate and direct impact, give your smile, time, connections, and support, or share your experiences, wisdom, and knowledge with others. This is often even more valuable than money itself.

"We give but little when we give up our possessions. It is when we give of ourselves that we truly give." –Khalil Gibran

If you are holding on to a lot of things that you do not need nor enjoy, and you have no emotional attachment to them, give them away!

Donate them or sell them to someone who can use them.

Why is this so important? You want to own your things and not be owned by them.

Fix what is broken, clean what is dirty, and sell, donate, or dispose of what no longer serves you, in your mind, body, heart, and home.

How do you leave a legacy? Plant a seed and watch it grow.

Make the days in your life count by giving back.

Become the pebble thrown into the pond, and let it ripple through.

Here are a few suggestions:
- Open a door for someone.
- Open your home (and your heart).
- Listen to someone who would otherwise be lonely.
- Pay for someone's meal.
- Visit people without relatives in the hospital, bring flowers or a small gift, but most of all, a smile and compassion.
- Take food and clothing to a home in need.
- Donate part of your holiday money, or give presents or food to a charity, for people who have far less than yourself.
- Pay a child's tuition for one full year. Depending on the country, this might cost little compared to your income.
- Buy some of the supplies a charity home needs every day: toilet paper, soap, rice, here is an excellent example of asking what your recipient needs.
- Volunteer your time or transportation.
- For a struggling single parent, cover one month of day care, rent, or health insurance.
- Read to a lonely senior citizen, offering warmth and attention.
- Teach a child (who is not yours) a great skill that you have.
- Help in soup kitchens or with community projects.
- If you want to make a difference with your company and work, have a look at B1G1 online. I have seen the founders build the company, and they are making a tremendous worldwide impact with their work.

Countless opportunities!

Giving starts with kindness. To show kindness daily is the smallest of acts we can do to create change. Do something good for someone else today. And every day thereafter.

You will not lose but only gain.

There is one humanity.

We all have the exact basic human needs and emotions: water and food on our table, a roof over our heads, clothes on our bodies, education for our children, keeping our families safe, and a desire to make a decent life, and prosper.

"A generous heart, kind speech, and compassion are things which renew humanity." –Buddha

Legacy Questions

1. Do I know what **my purpose** is?
2. How am I **connected** to everyone else around me?
3. Do I know my **own boundaries**?
4. Where and how do I want to **contribute**?
5. How do I choose to **give back?**
6. What does **charity mean for me?** Giving of my resources such as time, money, products, knowledge, connections, information, work, energy, experience, knowledge, listening skills, and presence. Which one do I feel comfortable with? What am I uniquely suited for? What cause is important to me beyond self?
7. What do I want to be my **legacy**?
8. How do I **make it a reality**?

9. Who do I choose to **collaborate** with to make it a reality? Where can I get **support** for a specific project?
10. How do I want to create **ripples**?
11. How do I take **action** in my everyday life and immediate environment?
12. How do I choose to **make a difference** to someone else **each day** so that no day will be wasted?

6. Connection - The Currency of the Future

So far, there is only one humankind, one planet Earth, and one chance to get it right.

What does it all have to do with you?

Start at home and let your actions ripple from those nearest you to those across the planet.

At our core, we all have the same emotions and concerns: to love and be loved, accepted, respected, heard, and appreciated; to be part of a group, be it family, friends, colleagues or peers; to be seen as an individual.

We all seek happiness, health, safety, and well-being to certain degrees.

"When, indeed, shall we learn that we are all related to one another? That we are all members of one body." —Helen Keller

Oneness is about being connected to the whole. No one is an island; we do not exist in or by ourselves alone!

Here are a few questions to help you explore how you personally connect to your environment:

1. How do you feel about being a part of this life at this time?
2. What is influencing your life and its outcomes? (Consider the conditions you face, political, historical, cultural, and environmental.)
3. Where and how do you wish to fit on this planet?
4. What is your current role? Which role would you prefer?
5. What are your objectives and priorities in your community?
6. How do you celebrate unity through rituals, cultural events, and gratitude?

These are important questions because human beings are wired to be social.

We need regular interaction with others to stay sane and healthy.

Loneliness is not a natural state. It can be part of an acquired pattern.

You can fall into the habitual trap of thinking that you do not deserve to be loved or acknowledged.

We need bonding, emotional support, and connection to feel whole and healthy. Meeting people, learning how to communicate, and improving our social skills effectively are keys to achieving connection.

What Do You Want from Connection?

What is it that you want? Become aware of where and how you can best relate to others. This allows you to find and connect with like-minded people.

Go find your professional and personal tribe you can relate to.

Go online to find the groups interested in your favorite topic or who are likewise dedicated to solving the challenges that you choose to face every day.

Connecting with dynamic people who share your interests have never been easier.

If you feel lonely, take action.

Asking for advice, seeking help, and joining groups jolts us out of self-pity. It allows us to move forward with what and who we desire.

"If you want a certain thing, first be a certain person. Then, obtaining that certain thing will no longer be a concern." – Zen Proverb

A very good question to consider when you feel down and isolated is: *Are my needs covered?*

Check first if you might be suffering from a physical imbalance such as dehydration, poor nutrition, not enough sleep, too few breaks, too little socializing, not enough exercise, or the mind stuck in loops and worries or you are highly stressed and in need of some relaxation, meditation, priority and goal setting. You might need a different environment altogether.

Before you seek it elsewhere, check first above points.

Ensure you have taken care of all your basic needs first; with attention and willpower, you can remedy them one by one. Often, it takes simple steps to get back in balance.

Facing a gap in your nutrition and self-care, you would imbibe electrolytes, eat healthy meals, sleep seven to eight hours a night, take a day or a weekend off, meet with people who recharge your batteries, exercise, and do an activity you enjoy.

It is possible to bring all of these into your weekly routine, which will help you learn how to tame your mind and moods. One step at a time may lead you to astonishing results.

It cannot be overstated; self-awareness is the key to maintaining your well-being!

Your brain, body, and soul need the appropriate fuel AND maintenance to function, act, and thrive properly!

Choice
Live by choice - not by chance!
Make changes - not excuses.
Be motivated - not manipulated.
Be useful - not used.
Excel - not compete.
Self-esteem - not self-pity.

Listen to your inner voice not the random opinions of others.

There are few things more rewarding than knowing that your work and your presence is making a positive impact, not just on yourself but also on the entire system you are a part of.

Connection Questions

1. **Who** do I want to be in this world?
2. How do I get out of **isolation**?
3. How do I deal with **loneliness and separation**?
4. How do I choose to **connect** to everything else?
5. How am I a part of the whole, my family, community, culture, society, humankind, the planet?
6. How do I want to **connect** to others **on a personal level**?
7. How can I develop my **empathy**? Emotional bonding and awareness of all my senses.
8. How do I give **kindness?**
9. How do I **forgive and move on**?
10. How am I connected to something **bigger than myself**?
11. How do I choose to create reality beyond just my own personal needs?
12. How am I connected to a **greater power**?
13. How do I have **faith**?
14. How do I create **my reality**?
15. How do I develop **trust** in life?
16. How do I value **honesty** with myself and others?
17. How do I find a **belief** that is constructive for my life and others?
18. Do I consciously choose and create my **environment**?
19. Uncluttering and letting go through all levels are powerful tools in transition periods to create forward

momentum. Let go first, then receive and welcome the new, it doesn't work the other way round.

7. Business - Your Reflection

Mind your own business.

Before we venture into starting a business, we need to clearly define our motivation for *why* we want to do it.

Specifically:
— We need clarity on the **purpose** of the business and our vision for it.
— The **actual needs** and wants of the clients and markets (not just our own needs and wants).
— The required **structures, strategies,** and **financing**.

Make sure to check facts, figures, and actions, not promises and wishes!

What Is Your Business IQ?

Running your own business takes knowledge and skills that are often unrelated to the technical part of what you do, which is your expertise. Excellent professionals have great technical jobs, yet when they start their own business, they tend to find themselves overwhelmed with all the tasks required as well as the demands of becoming their own boss.

All our days only have 24 hours! There is only that much one can do.

However, there are *countless* skills required to successfully run a business, as well as your own life.

As an employee, most likely you enjoyed a whole depart-ment, and at least a team, tasked with doing the work that makes a business run.

In a startup, YOU will do it all!

Entrepreneurs find themselves on their own, certainly in the beginning, in an endless sea of challenges.

Even the smallest tasks pull at them to the detriment of everything else. As a business owner or even solopreneur, you are wrenched in different directions until you create, with blood, sweat and tears, a qualified team, structure, and financing.

These are the key (soft) skills you will need:
- Self-management
- People management
- Awareness of working styles, needs, and personality types.
- How to collaborate with people smarter than you in your field.
- Delegating, instead of trying to do everything yourself, saves valuable time, resources, and energy. You do not have to reinvent the wheel! Beware: Delegating does not mean just dumping tasks on someone else, but guidance and collaboration to solve a challenge more effectively together.

As a new entrepreneur, you will be tied up learning, constantly exploring new knowledge and opportunities, and striving to consciously understand and master your own emotions and fears, mindset, skills, and habits as a part of the necessary personal development process as a business *owner*.

This is and means taking on full responsibility for your life, all that this book is really about.

Marketing and Sales

How are you going to get clients, and how do you ensure they will pay you adequately? Finding clients, reliably, who will pay for the services or goods you deliver is imperative.

You will need to know yourself, your value proposition, the target demographic, and your client base.

Clients are looking for experts in their field with a track record of success and their respective credentials. These are built over time, step by step.

People do business with professionals they like and trust and with whom they enjoy a positive interaction and history!

That is where your relationship-building skills come in. To start, find and focus on a small niche. This will greatly help you land the right clients, and help the right clients find you.

If you cannot sell, there is no point in trying to start a business.

You need to be able to sell yourself, your product or service, and your business as a capable entrepreneur and to survive.

You have to be able to sell your ideas, vision, numbers, and product or service to your team members, investors, clients, and sponsors.

People do not buy your product, they buy YOU and your story!

The feelings you evoke and the hope of profits or a specific advantage *for them* that you can give.

Knowing what you have going for yourself in ability, skill, talent, experience, business acumen, and especially grit is a key ingredient required before venturing out on your own.

Indispensable entrepreneurial skills to work and improve

- A very strong work ethic.
- Resilience.
- Excellent communication, listening, and interpersonal skills.
- Strong problem-solving skills.
- Time and stress management skills.
- Ability to delay gratification.
- Flexibility.
- Independent working skills.
- High self-motivation.
- Computer and technology skills.
- Project management skills.
- Unshakeable self-confidence and self-esteem.
- Grit and perseverance.
- Ability to accept constructive criticism.
- Enforcing boundaries.

- Strong research and learning skills.
- Adaptability and an open learning mindset.
- Knowing the rules of the game and having proper business structures.
- Market research, marketing, sales, psychological business knowledge, client acquisition and retention skills, and organizational development skills.
- Accounting, tax, and financing knowledge.
- Understanding of logistics.
- Awareness of laws and regulations.
- And many more.

Building the Winning Team

It is so important to find partners and build a team that aligns with your vision, values, and belief system.

"Talent wins games, but teamwork and intelligence win championships." –Michael Jordan

Why are people so important?

There is no such thing as "self-made," we only reach our goals with the help and collaboration of others!

Remember: A team is **always** stronger than just one person alone.

Success is a team sport!

Each of us has only 24 hours per day.

No matter how brilliant and experienced we are:

1. There will always be more to do than we can do in a day.
2. There will always be something that we *should not* be doing that someone else *can be* doing.

Focus on your strengths and outsource the rest.

How Do You Create Your Business Systems?

Look at the existing, successful systems around you for examples. Chances are, someone else is already doing what you want to achieve.

Partner with them. Join forces and channel your time, energy, and resources.

This allows you to multiply the outcome of your efforts and increase your authority and credibility substantially!

Do You Really Need a Co-founder?

If you are looking for a co-founder to minimize the risks, ensure that you need the person's skillset!

Do not make a rash decision because you like him or feel enamored with his potential 'superpowers.'

Sincerely ask yourself:

"Would I give up to 50 percent equity in my company if I could just hire someone to do the same thing?"

Focus on Your Strengths

Focus on your strengths and *outsource the rest*. You will thrive.

Put money first; you will lose people.

Put people and their success first, and you will meet and keep great people. This is how companies become successful!

Build a network and find accountability partners through online platforms and company websites. A precise online search with GenAI Agents will quickly show the relevant contacts to approach.

Inexpensive support can be internationally hired on the spot as needed through online platforms. These offer a whole range of services, from virtual assistants, executive assistants, bookkeeping, secretary services and more to create and design your work environment. . The AI space is developing at lightning speed! Many of the repetitive tasks can be automated altogether.

Stay relevant and learn how to leverage latest developments. Awareness is key!

Avoid Overhead Costs

If you are a startup, it pays to avoid the overhead costs for office space, equipment, fancy design, and employees. These truly can wreak havoc on the bottom line. Work from home or try a collaborative co-working spaces, where you can rent rooms and infrastructure that you might need short term. Avoid spending as much as you can and rely on free online services, personal network resources, and highly effective and efficient platforms, making your life a lot easier. Automate processes as much as you can and create scalable systems that do not require your physical presence.

Marketing materials or your website evolve and change over time. Do not waste too much time on these initially – you are your company's best marketing tool. Look and walk the talk. Connect with networks and prospective customers. Reach out and ask for introduction meetings.

The key is to network and put yourself out there!

Just. Get. Started!

Delegate.
Communicate.
Ask.
Learn.
Adapt.
Grow.
Adjust.
Expand.
Pivot.
Keep going.
Ask for help, often!
Network!

It is not about whom you know, but who knows (about) you!
Your net worth is in your network!

Work with mentors, role models, and professional advisors.

Joint venture for wider reach, immediate upgrade of your credibility and expansion of your networks!

Grow by affiliation to those having walked the talk.

Before Managing People

Before managing others, have a tight grip on your mind, on how you operate, self-awareness, and deep self-knowledge.

Investing in your own personal growth, skill and under-standing *first*, will help you to avoid costly mistakes in business *later*.

Find a strategy and a mentor who you can connect with and learn from. This book is a first step in the right direction.

Look for like-minded professionals with whom you can part-ner in some form. Collaborate with people who are ahead of you, and you will move much faster to where you want to go.

Legals

Get a good lawyer's advice on business transactions *before!* venturing into deals!

- Get your legal structures set up correctly!
  Believe in actions, numbers, and figures, not words, promises, and marketing!

- Always put agreements in writing to reconfirm what you discussed and summarize communications via e-mail. Leave a 'paper trail'.
  Send important documents via secure online platforms, registered mail, or express delivery to the recipient . Keep copies; do not lose the receipts!

These points are non-negotiable if you want to be safe, and not sorry.

Business is business; family and friendship are family and friendship, it is highly advisable not to mix the two.

Hedge against the risk of things falling apart if things go South.

Speed and Accuracy

You are learning to swim, so…you are going to get wet!

Overthinking and wanting to get everything perfectly right will slow down your momentum tremendously, work speed, and the learning that only comes from making a sale, shipping a product, or performing your service.

Overthinking, a telltale sign of fear, will halt your process, lead to procrastination, and inhibit your success.

No amount of theory and analysis will teach you how to stay afloat!

Practice, trial, and error are the pathways to an eventual successful outcome.

They are inevitable if you do not quit.

To succeed: fail faster. Everyone who is successful has failed, many times!

Each time will provide valuable lessons, knowledge, and insights that cannot be gained just by reading books!

Putting knowledge into action and gaining experience carries you forward to your goals.

Never fall into the mind trap that failure is the end of your journey!

After you fail, focus on getting back up, dust yourself off, and taking **consistent** actions while keeping your big vision in mind. This is what will bring results and income.

Get going; you can always adjust, change, alter, or expand your approaches on the go.

In entrepreneurship, doing a flawed project is far better than doing nothing perfectly.

The Fear of Having Nothing or Losing It All

Because failure is inevitable, and the speed of business is not always on your side, always keep doing what pays you, and create a safety net of a few months cashflow in reach.

If this is not an option, do not start a business. It takes money to make money.

How do you handle not having enough?

You will almost certainly have times when the money you need is not there (yet) at that moment.

At that point, remember this:

Whenever the fear of lack arises within you, remain focused, stable, and grounded despite the panic you might momentarily feel, do the breathing exercise and focus on the next one action to take to move things forward.

Remember that you are not your bank account. You are not your business.
You are not your possessions.

You have them! This realization is essential.

Remind yourself that all you essentially need is your health, a roof over your head, food on the table, clothes on your body, and shoes on your feet, and the same with your family.

As long as the basics are covered, you are ok!

The breathing exercise will help you to move through feelings of fear and take action instead.

Remember, if you are safe and enjoy a comfortable bed to sleep on, you are already better off than most people in this world.

Keeping this in mind helps to keep your emotions and fears in check.

You are not your circumstances! They will always change and so will you!

Remember, too, that you are **investing** in yourself.

You are not failing because your fortunes are down; rather,

- you are making yourself knowledgeable
- improving in the areas where you are lacking building collaborations and joint ventures
- work with great people who are ahead of you and believe in you

These are simply the growing pains as you rise to meet your goals.

"Repetition – we are what we repeatedly do!

Excellence is not an act, but a habit." –Aristotle

Life Integration: How Not to Fail Too Hard

There is failure, and then there is a failed business. A startup brings its very own challenges and demands.

Often as not, certain demands are at odds with business survival and present owners with an irreconcilable catch-22. Hence, it is no surprise that most businesses fail within the first two years!

Those years can be gut-wrenching for founders and owners with the highest stress levels, with sleepless nights, very long and irregular work hours around the clock, steep learning curves, and being consistently challenged to perform at maximum at many different levels.

Despite these expectations, it is crucial to strive to integrate all your life areas, so you can stay safe and healthy.

Just being busy does not equal results or a successful outcome.

This is a trap that many of us fall into out of anxiety or when we need to feel important.

Your company, and even your employees, are never worth developing serious health issues over due to extended periods of high stress!

Listen to the signs your body sends you!

Taking a break, going for a walk outside in nature, and spending time with your friends and family are crucial for your continued well-being!

Your relationships need time and nurturing.
Many push them to the side, focusing solely on the business.
This is a very bad choice as the work stream is endless!

Yet we cannot replace time spent with our family and our loved ones!

You can always find time for what you really want or need to do.

Make how you spend your time a smart choice.

Otherwise, one day, you might wake up to the realization that you have sacrificed *everything* for the idea you pursued, for the sake of making more money and losing everything else in its wake.

Be careful. Pay attention!

To go fast, go slow, sustainable, and steady. Mentally, learn *how to vet opportunities.*

The capability to say 'no' is your first line of defense, what you say no to saves your time and life energy.

Great entrepreneurs are *excellent at setting, enforcing,* and *protecting* their boundaries!

Out of 100 things to do, only say yes to the 1-2% that move you and your business forward.

Learn as much as you can to make smart choices. Collaborate, outsource, and delegate as much as you can.

This crucial survival skill will ensure that you do not run out of time, motivation, energy, health, or funds.

Less is more.

Evaluating and saying "no" so-called "opportunities" is an absolute must!

People think focus means saying 'yes' to the thing we have got to focus on. But that is not what it means at all.

It means saying no to the hundred other good ideas that there are.

"We have to pick carefully. Keep it simple."
–Steve Jobs

Creating and Giving Value

Business is about delivering what people need and want! You are creating value when you solve a *real* problem.

The question is not: "What can we get from you?" but "What can we *do* for you?"

This demands us to be more interested in the solutions we offer and less interested in fulfilling our personal needs first when we work with people and companies.

Ideally, the *strength and reach* of your solution for many will take care of what you need!

To that end, the more people you can serve with your services or products, the more money you will make.

According to Robert Kiyosaki, for a business to become successful, it needs a triangular system:

1. Team
2. Leadership
3. Mission

They all share equal importance.

Inside the triangle are the tools, stacked from the top to the bottom of the triangle, in ascending order of importance:

1. Product
2. Legal
3. Systems
4. Communications
5. Cash flow

Not surprisingly, cash flow is the largest sector and forms the foundation.

All these points have to be clear and in place.

If any of these parts are missing or neglected, the business IS going to fail.

Further, Kiyosaki puts people into four work categories of increasing power:

1. Employed
2. Self-employed
3. Business Owners
4. Investors

Each of the categories has its very own mindset and a required set of skills, knowledge, and experience.

Many entrepreneurs create **self-employment**. Instead of working *on* their business, they are working *in* their business 24/7, trading their valuable time for money.

This approach has extremely limited growth potential and is *not* scalable!

They soon find themselves stuck, time-scarce, exhausted, and with insufficient resources, and eventually, insufficient health.

What to do?
Focus on what generates revenue and do more of what works!

Read or watch biographies of good business role models who can inspire you to follow in their footsteps and define your own strategies.

Hearing, reading, and seeing what other people have gone through to acquire their knowledge and experience, achieving success is key.

Don't reinvent the wheel, learn and adapt what worked for them!

They were hungry to grow, both personally, and in their endeavors. They mustered the courage to pursue their goals every day over extended periods of time, years, and even decades. They recovered from setbacks, overcame hurdles and tremendous challenges, taking consistent actions toward reaching their goals.

What Is Your Value Proposition?

Do you know your value proposition and how it relates to someone else's problem?

Can you perform the calculations, reassure productivity dividends, minimize lost opportunity costs, and ensure whatever it takes to get a sale and service your potential client?

To find solutions, think outside the box, and use creative, unusual, yet legal approaches.

Brainstorming with a wide variety of people will give you unconventional ideas and results. Artists, teachers, and psychologists often see the world very differently from lawyers, engineers, accountants, or scientists.

Have conversations with all of them! You will create valuable insights for your own business to learn how to tackle challenges from different points of view and angles.

Focus. Keep your energy high and your mind clear.

Consider cutting what drains you unnecessarily. Certain people, situations, environments, tasks, expenses, habits, or social activities can be neglected if they do not add significantly to your well-being and mental health.

Starting a business is already hard enough. Don't get distracted by things that drain you!

Nurture your essential relationships, activities, health, and well-being.

Everything else. . .Declutter.

Learn how to say no, setting and, most importantly, enforcing boundaries and sticking to them, overcoming the fear of becoming unpopular.

Success is not for the fainthearted!

Set your inner GPS on reaching your best possible outcomes.

Be happy. Communicate, negotiate, and if no results are achieved, walk away.

The power to say no sends a very clear message!

Not just to who you are turning down, but to *yourself* in terms of self-respect.

Work with a licensed therapist to accelerate your self-awareness and your learning curve and to cover blind spots.

How to Deal with the Inner-Depressed Entrepreneur

We all tend to forget what makes us happy and feel good in times of stress and high pressure!

If not careful in enforcing boundaries with yourself and others, it is easy to burn out.

Never be too busy making a living that you forget to live…

When you feel down, it helps to check in on all the personal points in Chapters 1–6 and strive to keep them balanced.

It will not always be possible, yet the key is to reset every time to your solid baseline that benefits your overall health.

> Keep within reach a journal or list of what makes you feel good. Ideally, things that you can do by and for yourself.
>
> I call it your 'personal house pharmacy.'
>
> Read through it when you are feeling low and do one of them immediately. It will help greatly to orientate yourself back to your north.

This will be invaluable in rough times.

Combine it with the three-minute breathing exercise, and it will open enough space in your mind to make immediate daily self-care a priority.

On your journey, you have one job: Setting one foot in front of the other and just keeping going.

No one jumps up a mountain!

Step by step, you will be able to reach your goals with steady focus and taking informed actions.

"The journey of a thousand miles begins with one step."
—Lao Tzu

Building Legal Structure and Getting Insurance

Nobody likes fighting for what is rightfully theirs or going to court. But, if we do not protect ourselves legally, we will be taken advantage of left, right, and center.

Learn, from the best legal advice you can afford, how to legally structure your business and collaborations.

Remember, just because you have a contract, it does not mean you are protected.

Without sufficient time, energy, counsel, and resources to enforce it, it is a lost case, even if the law is on your side.

You will make legal and financial mistakes. You will fail.

Failure is an integral part of doing business and, ironically, of becoming successful. Experience and wisdom are earned, not given.

This is one of the reasons why you should never invest all your money back into your own business! Pay yourself first. Reduce living costs as much as you can, cover essentials, and save!

The key question here is: how fast can you recover from setbacks and failures?

Don't give up.

Hearts bend. They don't break, even if it feels like it at times. Life isn't over until it is over.

With acceptance healing over time becomes possible. Setbacks are stepping stones to new learning and greater successes.

Keep going!

Unless quitting or going at a slower life pace truly makes more sense for major reasons: health, loved ones, and keeping your sanity and your family together.

There is no age limit at which you can start a business.

There will always be new opportunities out there for born entrepreneurs.

Yet at certain times in life, it might just not be what we are meant to do if we are truly honest with ourselves, leaving the ego aside. It is okay wanting to have a happy family and a personal life and be less stressed, especially if they do not support you in your endeavors. Do not throw the baby out with the bathwater.

Trusting People?

Do not trust people blindly in life or business.

In many parts of the world, people think if someone gets ripped off, they deserve it for being so stupid.

Yet know that getting cheated on or ripped off happens to everybody at some point in life, no matter how smart a person is.

Hearing "It is just business, no hard feelings" is a weak comfort when you are the one losing out.

> If you have *doubts* that you can trust someone, *do not trust them.*

Even if it all looks great on paper, if your gut is telling you that something is off, but you cannot put a finger on it, listen to your gut instinct!

Do not let reason interfere and override your intuition. Your gut instinct is usually right.

Take Time to Reach a Decision

Take time to get the facts right and make accurate decisions.

Determine ahead of time the needs and requirements of each situation.

Problems rarely drop out of the sky but build up over time.

Pay attention to the small indicators to avoid the bigger issues later down the road.

This is not always possible, yet it is an excellent point to keep in mind and be aware of.

As the famous Spanish artist Salvador Dali said: *"Have no fear of perfection—you will never reach it."* Further, we have to become aware of:

- our excuses
- perfectionism
- fear
- controlling and fixed mindset
- toxic people
- people pleasing
- and saying yes when we would rather say no.

People will always think what they want to think, regardless of our actions.

Look out for red flags and change your (inter) actions accordingly.

If respect is not served, leave the table.

Be Kind to Yourself

Your goals are progress, improvement and self-reflection. Not just "Success."

Be kind to yourself in the process, as we are all on this learning path called life together. Do not compare your progress to other people; take action and be patient. If people tell you something can't be done, take it with a grain of salt. They are not in your situation nor in your shoes, nor do they have your vision, mission, and goals as a priority in their life.

It also helps to love what we do. Otherwise, we will be unlikely to pull through long working hours and massive challenges along the way.

If you spend your workdays doing things you hate, life will pass you by in a blink. Eventually, you will feel bitter, empty, angry, and miserable for having missed out on a great experience.

When we look back, people usually regret the things that they did not do in their life for whatever reason, although they desired to.

We can get over failures by having put in the effort and tried our luck. Yet we rarely get over missed chances and opportunities when they presented themselves to us and for whatever reason, we did not go for them out of fear, doubts, insecurity, or worse, because we let others talk us out of it.

So, choose what you do, and who you do it with, wisely!

"Luck is a dividend of sweat. The more we sweat, the luckier we get." –Ray Kroc

Goal Setting

Clear, detailed goal setting is very important to know what you want to achieve and by when.

It creates simplicity and a structure to follow.

A clear focus of the mind allows the "how" to appear, and you will find that opportunities open before you.

Business is a constant learning curve.

Be open and humble enough to *un*learn and *re*learn (many times) and to listen to a variety of viewpoints.

Like Zig Ziglar famously said: "You will get all you want in life if you help enough other people get what they want."

To explore and discover unfamiliar territories, read and study as much as you can. Talk to mentors, coaches, advisors, and professionals ahead of you. Do your research.

Partner with professionals who bring in skills that you lack to your business.

Listening

The only way to determine the needs of your clients is to truly listen.

Misplaced pride, ego, and arrogance can become your downfall. In an ever-faster 24/7-connected world, the competition is stiff and global!

After you have lost the client, reflect on why and do a thorough and honest self-analysis; this will help you grow and develop further.

Your attitude and humility are the highest-priced currency in the market. It is what will determine whether you will succeed. Taking positive action means accepting responsibility constantly, overcoming fear, and letting go of sarcasm, irony, spite, blame, and self-pity.

It means becoming 100 percent accountable.

Live, breathe, and personify your positive beliefs and values, serving others with humility and gratitude.

This is hard work!

Taking true responsibility in business is always a conscious decision and a lifelong journey.

"Before we can understand, manage, and lead others, we first have to understand, manage and lead ourselves." –Paul J Myer

A former Medical Research Director at one of the world's largest pharmaceutical companies, summed this up with the following:

"See and bring out the best in people. Understand that every one is in the world to learn. Allow mistakes they are a good thing. Making them fast and learning from them is a more powerful thing than living in fear of them. Change is the only constant in life; in 50 to 100 years, we will not be here. Be brave, a good person, and help others.

Everyone wants to do well, be respected, and learn.

Make decisions, take risks, be responsible, accountable, and stand for the decisions you make."

Business Questions
1. Do I **mind my own business and my own life first**?
2. What is my **niche** and **specialty**?
3. Do I have what it takes and **how do I get it**?
4. Do I **keep learning** every day?
5. Do I **collaborate** with people who are already **successful** in what I want to do?
6. Do I work **on** my business? (Not in my business, having created another job for myself?)
7. Is there an **equal exchange** in our collaboration?
8. Do I **share** information, ideas, and data?
9. Do I come in my mindset from a place of **abundance** or scarcity?

10. Do I have the **proper legal structures** for my business? Do I **legally protect** my business and my name?
11. What is the **culture** I want to have in my business? How do we **communicate** it **clearly** and **concisely**?
12. Do I **keep** time, resources, and energy between **personal and business separate**, especially in a startup?
13. Do I **fulfill** clients' and the market's real **needs**, not just my ego?
14. Do I know about **trends and markets**?
15. Do I offer **solutions** to real problems?
16. Do I **focus on** one **niche** and become great at it?
17. Do I create or join **networks** of like-minded professionals?
18. Do I **love** what I do? Am I **passionate** about what I do?
19. Do I create **trust**? How am I t**rustworthy**?
20. Do I **think out of the box**?
21. Do I **ignore** the negative inner voices and outer naysayers?
22. How do I deal with **failure** and **success** and ask myself: What is next?
23. How good am I at dealing with **uncertainty** and taking focused actions, regardless?
24. How strong is my **self-motivation** and **self-discipline**?
25. How do I **reinvent** myself?
26. What do I know about and how good am I at hiring, **teamwork** and people management?
27. **Do I understand and communicate complexities,** common points, vision, mission, and goals?
28. Do I know my **value** proposition relative to someone else's problem?

8. Finance - Money Management

People who understand how to handle money live more successful lives.

You cannot steer, direct, and oversee your finances if the only thing you know about money is how to spend it!

Becoming financially fit is a necessary survival skill, which, unfortunately, is still not taught in school and is often over-simplified on social media.

What if you do not like numbers and financial details?

You will *not* get around this one if you want to be in charge of and get ahead in your own life.
Analyze your finances. Numbers do not lie.

Know Your Numbers!

- Learn the basics and the vocabulary, online, from books and in classes. Avoid get-rich-quick schemes! To start, learn the solid basics by reading one small article about the economy and money every day.
- Create a budget, track all your expenses, and know where your money goes to be able to steer your expenses toward what you want to achieve.
- Gain a solid knowledge of your finances, habits, and weaknesses. Become informed about what is yours to manage.
  Then, get a grip on it so you can learn how to invest it wisely.
- Aim beyond living paycheck to paycheck.
- Do not lend expecting money back! It will strain your relationship!
- Stop "just spending money" and start making income from various sources. There are plenty of opportunities out there.

- Pay off debts as quickly as possible, and only go into debt for things of long-term value such as property investments.

"Never take advice from someone regarding your finances who has or earns less than you do! You know they are good at it if they are rich." –Larry Winget

Money management skills and investment have a lot to do with self-education and development, gaining control over our skills, emotions, bodies, minds, and ourselves, and knowing how to deal with uncertainty and pressure.

Money comes and goes. As we breathe, or like waves of the sea, money comes in, and money goes out. Sometimes, losing it is the only way to learn how to handle money.

How fast you transition and bounce back from adversity will define your success.

When you make money, keep your own greed and irresponsibility in check and capitalize on opportunities.

Money management takes patience, discipline, and a lot of learning what *not* to do.

Wealth destruction is when capital goods, such as property equity, are used to pay for consumer goods.

Things like home remodeling, appliances, vacations, food and restaurants, partying, clothing, and cars.

Your children's education only happens once in life, make sure you get it right and invest in their proper upbringing. Later on, you won't be able to go back and redo what you missed out on.

Keeping your budget in balance takes great self-control and discipline!

You have needs, wants, and *urgencies*.

To juggle them, especially with limited funds, you must tighten your spending habits, or much better, generate more income!

"The tighter we squeeze, the less we have." –Ma-Tsu Tao-i

There are many tools available online that will allow you to:

1. Keep track of your expenses.
2. Review your expenses monthly.
3. Steer your spending habits in the healthiest direction, so you can cover your expenses, save, and pay your taxes and debts.

If one month you spend an excessive amount of money in a specific category, avoid doing the same thing next month to break the pattern.

The discipline of tracking expenses to create awareness and accountability matters.

Money Problems

We run into trouble when:

1. We only have one source of income.
2. Our cashflow is too low or slow.
3. We do poor forecasting.
4. Have locked-in assets, raising inventories and goods.
5. Too much debt.
6. Undercapitalization (not enough cash available.)
7. Liquidity crunch.
8. Experience of unforeseen life events.
9. Not having sufficient insurance in place,

You cannot plan for everything**, but it is advisable to have six months of cash saved for emergencies**.

"Dig the well before you are thirsty." –Chinese Proverb

The first step is to get your finances in order!

Do Not Quit Your Day Job

Keeping your job allows you to acquire positive cash flow, which is the money in your pocket *after* you have paid all your expenses.

Know Your Assets and Liabilities

Assets. These put money into your pocket.
Liabilities. These take money out of your pocket.

We will use them to calculate your net worth, which is what remains in the end under the bottom line.

Financially speaking, anything you do that is not putting money into your pocket is a *liability*, not an asset.

Your future gains are hypothetical, i.e., *not in your pocket*.

Just as the sale is not closed until you have the money in your bank account, so too, you cannot use the money "promised" or "expected" when forecasting your expenses.

Deal with what IS.

Create a Schedule of Assets and Liabilities

A schedule of assets and liabilities allows you to see clearly what you have and what you do not have.

Here is what it looks like:

Divide a spreadsheet into two main columns.

Your assets include your home value (if owned), personal effects, business interests, cars, cash, valuables, and investments.

On one side, list your assets, such as:

- Cash (cash in hand, current accounts, fixed deposit, savings accounts)
- Investments (stocks, bonds, mutual funds, corporate plans, employee provident funds)
- Real Estate (investment properties, not your home, which is not an asset if you live in it)
- Life insurance (cash value)
- Motor vehicles (current market value)

- Receivables (debtors; they owe you money)
- Other assets (household goods, jewelry, collections, art, and others)

Calculate the total of each category and then the grand total of all your assets. Face what IS.

Property is one of the very few assets that banks are willing to give loans against.

On the other side, we have liabilities:

- Real estate loans (housing, your own property, investment properties)
- Other loans (motor vehicles, other loans, company loans)
- Payables (credit cards, charge accounts, overdrafts, creditors)
- Other liabilities (income tax, other loans, contingent liabilities)

Calculate the total of each category. Then, the total of all categories together. Total **assets** *minus* total **liabilities** reflect your **net worth**.

Personal financial data is your grown-up report card!

The Golden Rule of Investing

Investments can go up, sideways, or down at any time!

Finding the investments that you feel comfortable with should be based on credentials, accreditations, facts, and figures, not on blindly investing what you cannot afford to lose!

The Mighty Multiple

Strive to create multiple streams of income over time and a diversified portfolio.

Here is a list of income instruments:

affiliations
commissions
joint ventures
royalties
dividends from blue chip stocks or certain types of insurances
crypto currencies
equities precious
metals
commodities
foreign exchange currencies
stock market and government bonds real
estate

Remember that equity from your real estate value is *not* money in your pocket! First, it is tied up. Second, just as investments can change, your equity can change when markets turn, political winds shift, or disaster strikes. Do your diligence and thorough research.

Learn which of these investment types suit your interests and skills. All of them require an investment of time and dedication to master, and it is worth it.

Educate yourself about the many types of investment opportunities. It is important to choose one you understand and can feel passionate about!

Be extra careful doing your due diligence with financial advisors and if an instrument is labeled as a hands-off investment (there is rarely such a thing)!

No one will ever care as much about your money and well-being as you do!

Also, invest the time to look for the needle in the haystack, such as principal and insurance-protected investments.

They do exist.

When everyone runs in one direction, go the other way!

The Advance Payment Rule

Never send full payment in advance to someone you do not trust and know! The risk of losing your money is very high.

The possibility of getting it back, even if you do have signed contracts, is very low. People like to get money; they do not like to part with it.

Make partial payments, such as 50 percent up front. Only pay the balance when they completed the job. . .*properly*.

This is especially true when you are working with contractors and solo operators.

Negotiate for project based and *avoid paying hourly fees*. The risk of unethical professionals dragging their feet to make an extra income is too high.

Always include as well that a contract can be cancelled without compensation if delivery and time frames fall short of

The Art of Investing

- Do not get emotionally attached to an investment.
- Buy low and sell high. Ideally, never sell if you want to accumulate wealth!
- If you invest in property, your money is tied up. Effectively, it does not exist. It is certainly not available for more profitable investments!
- Before investing in property, think of all the additional costs: property tax, upkeep, repair and maintenance, management fees, agent fees, insurance and mortgage costs, mortgage term assurance, sales and purchase agreement fees, holding and sales tax, closing costs such as legal fees, accountant fees, inflation, depreciation, and losses. Property agents rarely calculate these significant expenses in their return calculations! (Note that they are all tax deductible).
- Keep all your files in a very neat system for tax purposes and write offs. Many countries allow carrying forward tax credits to the next tax year or indefinitely. Inform yourself.
- Borrow money at fixed, not floating rates!
- If you get a guaranteed rental return, it is already calculated into the sales price. You are paying the returns to yourself out of your own pocket!
- Property appreciation and investment returns are never a given, no matter how rosy the possible returns are promised!
- Your own home or residence is not an investment if you live in it, because you pay and are responsible for all the expenses, unless you sublet to cover the costs.

"Do not save what is left after spending; instead spend what is left after saving." –Warren Buffet

- At times, it might be more profitable to rent your property, downgrade your lifestyle, and then invest the difference.
- Buying old real estate, renovating it and then selling it quickly can be attractive because it can be very profitable depending on country and property laws. Make sure you extensively inform yourself before investing! Learn the rules of the game before committing. Getting into investments is a breeze, getting out of them often a tedious process. Be careful what you say yes to!
- Flipping property is risky and only recommended for experienced high-risk investors. Timing your entry and exit from the investment is crucial. It also requires holding power and deep pockets. Mistakes and unpredictable market movements are unavoidable. now what you are doing, and have a banker, investors, contractors, a property manager, a lawyer, accountants, and a sales agent in place before working on deals. Before taking the plunge, learn the ropes by participating in programs or get experienced mentors guiding you through the steps.
- Property *development* takes real estate investment to a whole new level. Returns are considerably higher yet riskier. You may get there…start small, grow steady, learn consistently, and stay focused. Deals are structured upfront, bringing in investors into a company structure to develop projects.

There are many different types of investors.

We do not have to have millions to get started to build a portfolio, but we do have to do the research and acquire the knowledge of how the various investments work, the team, as well as the skills in how to invest successfully. The best investment is always in your own learning, progress, networks, and experience.

Read daily and learn about current events, especially as they relate to the jurisdictions, markets and the companies in which you are considering investing.

Only take advice from people who have walked the talk, who have achieved what you want to achieve, and who represent the values that are important to you.

Work with the best professionals you can afford and avoid taking business advice from your family and friends unless they are highly experienced in business, investment, family wealth, and legacy.

Think bigger.

You might have friends or colleagues who, like you, are interested in investment. Learn from them and share, but do not invest based on their advice without getting high-level insights.

Be careful of schemes: promised short-term big returns and interests, "hands off" investments, guaranteed returns, promised income or appreciation, they all require caution.

The wisest investments are comparatively. . .boring.

So are profitable businesses; they are, most of the time, anything but sexy.

Protect your finances and grow your wealth. Develop conscious spending habits!

Track your spending to ensure proper budgeting, check regularly on your debts, and reframe your perception of your net worth because it fluctuates constantly!

At the end of the day, it is not about how much money you *make* but how much you *keep* and *grow*.

Snapshots of Success Are Deceiving

In the long run, someone with a modest income, self-discipline, and no debts might be better off than a high roller with an extravagant lifestyle but huge debts to keep their costly infrastructure running.

Debts are good if they create higher revenue and increased value. Bad debts mean the money is lost forever with no returns.

Just because someone is making a fortune one year does not mean he will get to *keep* it.

If the skills of money management were never learned, (which is common among lottery winners and athletes), often going quickly broke, even with having millions in the bank.

Online and offline marketing is one reason why it is so common to spend recklessly.

Do not buy into the ads and marketing fads of what we supposedly need to buy to be happy.

The advertisers' primary objective is to get under our skin to sell us their products, which most of the time, we really do not need.

Real success is largely measured by how well you can protect yourself, your family, and your assets.

As a whole person, *health* is your biggest asset!

So is *love*, *time* spent with your family, and how you *contribute* to make a difference.

Applying for Financing

For expansion, eventually you will have to apply for financing or look for investors.

If you want to apply for a mortgage to buy a home, which for most is the biggest purchase that they will ever make, you will be asked to hand over the following information.

There is a lot of homework to be done, and forms you will have to complete.

This financing assessment process is an excellent tool for creating financial clarity even if you do not intend to get a mortgage.

Personal details include:
- your full (maiden) name
- date of birth (your age)
- home address
- phone numbers
- e-mail address

- relationship status
- nationality
- residence address (if renting or owning for collaterals)
- how long you have resided in this place
- previous address
- and if any foreseeable changes are pending

About Your Credit...

Your credit history is the basis on which you are judged loan-worthy.

It records if you have ever had a loan application refused, or if you have had a judgment for debt or loan default registered against you, failed to keep up with debt payments of any previous or current mortgages, rental or loan agreements, such as credit cards.

The lender will also want proof that you are good for the money. That you are financially capable of paying off the loan.

Employment is considered safe, controllable, and predicatble.

The lender will want to know:
- your employment status (employed, self-employed, contract worker, temporary, retired, business owner, investor, or other)
- the employment status of the joint applicant, if any
- current employer's name, address
- your occupation and job title
- how long you have been working for your current employer
- your national insurance or security number

- as well as the details of your previous employer if any.

Different countries have different rules and regulations, especially for entrepreneurs and startups!

It is worth relocating to get better terms and conditions including tax rates for starting your business. Do your research.

The way you structure upfront can give you a tremendous headstart to achieve a successful outcome! Consider tax rates, credits, grants, as well as social and economic safety, transportation, medical care, living costs, visa requirements for your passport, cultural values and weather conditions. Don't put your life at risk in catastrophe prone or highly dysregulated regions.

Avoiding Payment Shock

You cannot pay more than you can afford to generate.

Figure out what the amount is that you can handle!
- Assess your employment income over the last few years.
- Know your financial commitments, such as mortgage, rent, loan repayments, outstanding amounts, what you have to pay for utilities, such as gas, electricity, water, phone, taxes, health, insurance expenses .
- Next, consider what you spend on transportation, vacation, outstanding credit cards (outstandings can be consolidated and interests negotiated), regular savings, social activities, kids, education, yourself, and household expenses.

Your **net income** is what you make, minus all the expenses.

Define your **disposable income** per month to calculate how much you can afford on a mortgage payment.

Your credit worthiness also depends on your status as a buyer:
- if you are a first-time buyer
- moving
- remortgaging
- if you have a right to buy (laws and regulations)
- if it is a shared ownership scheme
- if it is for protection only
- borrowing on an additional account
- a buy-to-let property
- or let-to-buy
- a commercial mortgage
- a property development
- or if the property is located overseas

The bank will assess your current mortgages:
- the outstanding amount
- who is involved
- the type and interest to pay
- the repayment method such as capital repayment, interest only, or split arrangement
- if the terms are transferable
- are there early repayment charges?
- if we would be prepared to pay the charges to pay off the existing mortgage. (the lender gets far less interest due to early paying off). Be careful of penalties in case of early repayment when taking out a mortgage!

The bank may ask if you would like to consolidate your outstanding debts, such as loans and credit card bills, into your new mortgage to pay off the debts.

Consolidating your debts into your mortgage may reduce your monthly costs, but you will be paying these for a longer term, normally resulting in a larger overall payment!

You will also get to answer these questions. The realtor and a good mortgage broker will help give you this information:
- the lender will ask why you want a mortgage and assess what you can financially handle
- the address of the property to be mortgaged
- if you intend to live at that property
- the price and value
- the required loan amount
- the term of the mortgage
- if you wish to add other outstanding debt amounts
- the source of your funds in detail
- the number of rooms
- when the property was built
- if the property is of a non-standard construction (such as a usage or barn conversion)
- how long the property tenure will be if it is a freehold or leasehold title (and how long is left on the lease)
- the property type (house, bungalow, flat, condominium, or other)
- if any home improvements are planned (value increase of property)
- if the ownership is shared (to which percentage, as well as details of the scheme)

- and if you need to borrow an additional amount, plus the reasons why such as for a construction loan to increase the property value

Investment Is a Team Sport

Lists like the one above are important.

Even before you have all your financial data together, they help you invest in your education to acquire the knowledge to make informed decisions.

Do not blindly trust others! Learn enough to ask informed questions. You and your returns will never be in their first and foremost interest.

So, how can you find trustworthy professionals who are legally and officially qualified?

Ratings and referrals are a good start. So is a track record going back at least a decade!

Do the research to learn what informed questions to ask and what red flags to look out for!

There are many financial books and courses available that will teach you this knowledge. These days you can easily do research with GenAI Agents yet always verify the information!

The time and money you spend on gaining financial literacy will be by far less expensive than the losses incurred due to financial ignorance, scams or overspending.

Be aware that some financial advisors and insurance agents receive hefty upfront commissions for the sales of their products to you.

If they are unethical, they have little to no interest in looking after your needs, or your money when the sale is over.

Suddenly, you cannot reach them. Due to a disclaimer in the fine print, they have zero responsibilities for your losses. BUT, if you want to move your investment away from them, you will pay a penalty for early cancellation!

Pay great attention to the fine prints!

Avoid high fees and locked-in investments with penalties for early sales at all costs!

When markets stagnate or tumble, certain investment companies will still make money and profit with your investment with sideways trading or put options, while *you* shoulder the losses.

That is why it is highly advisable to look for ethical, certified, and longstanding experienced investment advisors.

They should have great referrals, from referral sources of trust, and ideally, 15-20 years of experience and great recommendations.

It cannot be overstated how crucial it is to check out their ratings, feedback, and history.

"To know the road ahead, ask those coming back." –Chinese Proverb

The safest way to learn, generally, is from genuine professionals and mentors who are *not* trying to sell you.

They will save you valuable time, energy, and money by avoiding costly mistakes, trials, and errors!

Always get information at source not from hearsay, motivation, inspiration, or false promises.

As in any relationship, actions speak louder than words!

Believe what you observe, not what you hear.

Stop making excuses for people and situations and accept what IS.

Teach Yourself About Money (and Teach Your Kids!)

Wealth is not easily achieved and is even harder to preserve over generations. It requires a lot of work, on yourself , your fears, knowledge, skills, and mindset, to make, protect, keep, grow, and maintain it.

That is why teaching our children beyond just saving and how to make and handle money properly is an absolute must!

- It speeds up their learning,
- It guards them from making costly mistakes in the future.
- Teaches them common sense, reasoning, good money and negotiation skills.
- They learn how to vet and deal with people, transactions, advisors and brokers when they are older.

- Personal development is equally important to be able to communicate clearly and enforce boundaries when and where required.
- Teach them the value they can create to make money. Money is not a finite resource but can be generated through bringing value to others. The more value you create, the more money you make.
- Share with them how leverage and entrepreneurship work.
- Teach them resourcefulness and problem solving skills, how to deal with pain, fear, uncertainty, delayed gratification, and how to manage expectations.

If you do not feel equipped enough, there are age-appropriate courses and individual classes dedicated to teaching you as well as your kids about finances.

This is one of the most valuable investments that you will ever make in your children's education!

Here are some ways that you can teach your children financial awareness:

- Create shared goals you will have to save up money for to achieve.
- Brainstorm and plan how each child can earn and leverage their own money.
- Hold weekly meetings to help them monitor their cash flow. This keeps the goals aligned and things transparent.
- Make it fun, and continuous adjustments.
- Set goals and 'promotion' plans for each quarter together.
- Add deadlines to goals, so they can achieve them.

- Define the core 10 questions for each of you and to-gether regarding your spending: who, what, when, where, how, with whom, how much time, money / effort, why, what's next?

Money is energy. It takes care of those who value, respect, and take care of it.

One important point many miss:

Cancel unnecessary subscriptions or automatic debits to stop financial leaks. Even small amounts add up to bigger sums over time.

Make *sustainable* lifestyle choices that you can easily afford!

With money, as in every area of life, be mindful, increase your knowledge, cash flow, and ultimately net worth.

"Ask for what you want and be prepared to get it." –Maya Angelou

With focus, systems, processes, mental and emotional discipline and determination, you will certainly get there.

Check your bank statements monthly and use your credit cards wisely.

Remember, your credit card is really a *'debt'* card!

Set and enforce boundaries with people who ask to borrow from you.

Be especially careful if you are a people pleaser! Crooks and scammers will show *no hesitation* nor remorse taking advantage of you or your situation.

In fact, in certain low trust cultures it is very common to think you deserve it if you fall for it.

Help people to help themselves, and keep yourself safe.

This doesn't concern just money but the way you are treated, talked to, manners, given attention, and so on.

Exit such relationships quickly like a bad investment the sooner the better to reduce the damage done.

The best is if they are avoided altogether.

Parenting a grown adult is *not* your job!

(Unless it professionally is). Nor is it to make excuses for them!

Stare reality in the face and move on.

Prenups and agreed on shared responsibilities have nothing to do with being in love but with being reasonable.

They are a legal precautionary measure to avoid scams and all sorts of asset destruction from irresponsible or divorcing partners to greedy relatives and more they are put into place for damage control and if agreed on, mutual peace of mind.

Family will always remain family including the good, the bad and the ugly.

Make sure you remember the good, and put solid measures that stick into place to deal with and prevent the bad.

The "Third-Generation Curse" is real: the first generation founders build, the second generation heirs preserve, yet fortune usually gets squandered by the third generation due to lack of work ethic, poor financial management, or changing economic conditions leading to a cycle where family fortunes are often lost by the third generation.

A wise tycoon highly aware of this fact, a Hong Kong property billionaire, passed down structures to protect his multi-billion fortune and to last for his family for 1,750 years!

It is proof of his character, a deep understanding of his descendants personalities, as well as carrying forward his long-term vision after his passing.

His relatives and descendants do and will continue to receive highly generous monthly allowances, yet can't squander or get their hands on his fortune.

If this is a blessing or a curse remains to be seen.

Imagine an ancestor looked out for you in AD 275!

Situations, laws, economies, circumstances, values, and history continuously change.

Insurance

Insurance is tricky because you never get it when you need it.

Assessing your insurance needs with a qualified profes-sional and getting appropriate coverage is an absolute must!

Insurance is about safety and security.

Being uninsured is never worth the risk. For example, an 18-year-old without a family does not need life insurance unless he wants to look out for his siblings and parents. However, for a 32-year-old with children it is a must.

Once you really need insurance in case of misfortune you can't get it.

Review all your current insurance plans.

Determine if you have sufficient coverage, especially when your personal circumstances have changed. If you have married, purchased real estate, had a baby, or your grown children are leaving the nest, in case of divorce or death, you need to adjust your insurance needs as well as your will structure!

> Annually, compare prices, terms, and conditions for your insurance.

Do this with every plan you can afford for: health, accident, critical illness, disability, loss of income, medical, house, personal liability, car, and professional insurance.

These are helping to keep you safe from dramatic bills in times of need, which would only add to distress.

You can buy insurance on anything.

Some are critical and non-negotiable to have. You need cover age for your home, car, property and valuables, personal liability, travels, and medical emergencies.

Choose insurance wisely, and compare not just the prices but the fine print in terms and conditions as well on a yearly basis!

It is less hassle to put in the work to inform yourself properly as compared to when you have an incident and do need the insurance but don't have it. It is a no-brainer; be at peace later.

Planning for the Future

Think about your future needs, such as children's education, retirement, your bucket list, and health care. Always plan in advance. Make goals and take serious, non-negotiable actions toward them.

Plan for unexpected events, such as illness, accidents, unemployment, or a natural or personal disaster.

Buy the best insurance you can afford and talk to an expert to help you decide on the best insurance in the jurisdictions you *need*.

If you have a family, you need a proper legal will and life insurance. This will ensure your earthly possessions go to the right place and cover your family's expenses if anything happens to you.

Mortgage term assurance is a great thing to have, so your loved ones are not left with huge property debts in case of your demise. The mortgage will be paid off in full if something happens to you.

Again, do not count on the property value to be cashed out, it can go up and down! Property is not a liquid asset.

Nothing in life lasts forever; make sure you have the proper structures in place to pass it on in the way of your intent.

Keep a file in a secure and trusted place with all your relevant details, documents, and access keys for the worst case scenario.

"What we possess, we lose." –Zen Proverb

What Is the Difference Between a Will and a Trust?

It is crucial to have the legal structures in place to protect your last wishes.

A **will** details your wishes but has no teeth to enforce them!

This is why if there is a dispute, your family might have to go to court to fight for the legal right to claim what is in your will.

This can take up to *two years or more* if there are multiple heirs who don't respect your will, and can't agree with each other

A trust until probate is necessary for your family's financial safety to allow access to funds until the inheritance questions are sorted out.

It ensures that your family has access to money before your last will is executed.

Types of Trust

A trust involves three parties:

1. You, the trustor.
2. The trustee(s), who agree to manage your assets as directed by the terms of the trust. This can be a legal company structure.
3. The beneficiaries who will receive the assets.

A **trust** in *itself is* a legal entity that ensures your property is passed immediately to your named beneficiaries after your passing. There are no legal fees, no probate court, and no chaos or greed tearing your family apart.

Setting up proper trust structures can be costly, yet if you do have the wealth and assets, it is an absolute must.

If you have the means, consider a **revocable discretionary trust** which is a more elaborate instrument. Depending on the country you reside in, different rules and structures exist. An **irrevocable living trust** cannot be changed.

Inform yourself with a qualified, experienced and specialized lawyer in the jurisdictions of your assets as well as your residency.

If you have wealth, you are taking every smart action possible to have both a detailed legal will and a trust structure holding your properties and business entities as well as a detailed inventory of all your assets.

This is how legacies are built and passed on from generation to generation, without having to count on heirs or extended family members' character, accountability, generosity, loyalty and responsibility or a lack thereof.

Where There Is a Will, There Is a Way

But if you *do not* have a will, your belongings and assets will be distributed or seized according to the law of the country *where the assets are located!*

Do not leave a legacy of chaos!

- Hire a reputable estate planner.
- Create a will, and potentially a trust.
- Keep copies of all the documents.
- Update the will and trust *yearly*, and as needed.
- Close down unnecessary structures. Give power of attorney the authorization to act legally on your behalf, only to the most trustworthy people!

To be prepared is to be at peace in case of emergencies and life-threatening circumstances, knowing that you did put all your affairs in order before you urgently needed to!

Peace of mind is the best state to be in on your way to recovery or in a worst case scenario, when you pass on

Doing the best you can for unforeseen circumstances is all that you can do.

We Have Come Full Circle

"Only the crystal-clear question yields a transparent answer."
–Zen Proverb

You began reading this book by making sense of what you were given by your parents and ancestors, your life

In the end, everything that you build and built, the results of your success, will be passed on to the people you love or the causes that you care about.

Decide now what you want to pass on to them and what is going to be your legacy.

Raising self-sufficient, empowered, rooted, healthy, and confident children is the biggest gift in life you will give to them!

'A bird sitting on a tree is never afraid of the branch breaking, because its trust is not on the branch, but its own wings.'
–Anonymous

Finance Questions

1. What are my **thoughts** about money? How is my **relationship with money**? Whose **beliefs** did I take over? Do they serve my well-being? Do they empower me

and keep me safe and growing? Do I **choose** to keep or change them?

2. How **worthy** of money do I feel?
3. Do I invest in myself and my children by learning about money?
4. What shape are my current finances in? Do I regularly check on income, expenditures, debts, taxes, and savings?
5. Do I create a track record of successfully handling my finances and **debts?**
6. How d o I ensure we have enough **financial liquidity?**
7. Do I know where my money goes each month? What is my **cash flow**?
8. Do I know how to make the right choices for **budget, assets,** and **liabilities**? What do I need to **learn**?
9. What is my **net worth**?
10. Do I know how to **keep and protect money,** and make it **grow**? How to increase various streams of **income**?
11. Do I review my **insurance** plans and make sure I have sufficient coverage for health, disability, death, personal accident, house, car, travel, liability, professional, and life insurance?
12. What are my **major milestones in life,** and how do I financially plan for and **protect** them? Study, housing, marriage, children, university education, savings, lifestyle, travels and dreams, retirement, end of life.
    Set a timeline to move into taking focused action on a short (one year), mid (three years), and long (five to ten years) term timeline.
13. Do I invest in **sustainable lifestyle choices** and a healthy environment every day practicing self-care?
14. Do I know how to **use debt strategically,** such as mortgages on properties?

15. What do I know about the various types of **investments**?
16. Which type of **investment vehicle** is appealing to me? How do I make assets work for me?
17. Where can I learn about investments and businesses? How do I develop my **investment knowledge** and instincts? Start today and improve over time.
18. How do I choose good **mentors** and **advisors**?
19. Do I **let go** of bad decisions or deals and cut the losses and opportunity costs to be free to move on and focus on more beneficial endeavors?
20. Do I **make money work for me**, not the other way around? What automated **systems** and **processes** do I create?
21. How much do I **value my (life) time**? How **efficiently** do I use my **time**? How do I get **compensated** for my invested time?
22. Do I think in terms of **opportunities** instead of needs?
23. How do I create **abundance** in my life?
24. How quickly am I able to **implement** and **take focused action** in times of uncertainty? How quickly can I pivot to **move forward**?
25. How do I **protect** my money?
26. Do I learn the **basic language and vocabulary**? Finance Management - Investment Management - Portfolio Management - Project Financing - Key Areas - Investments and Returns (ROI) etc
27. Do I **review** my **financial plans** and situation **regularly** to adjust and improve them, putting the next action plans in place?
28. Do I have access to qualified **professional advice from highly experienced and officially certified** lawyers, accountants, bankers, mortgage brokers, financial advisors, insurance agents, property managers, tax accountants, investment, and other specialists, where required?

Can I research it online, through GenAI, recommendations or in groups?
29. How **grateful** am I for all that I *do* have?

What to Do with What You Have

There is so much to do and so little time.

So always believe in yourself. Under-promise and
over-deliver.

Your knowledge and experience are acquired over your entire
lifetime. Their combination is uniquely yours. Value them!

A short story :

"A ship engine failed, no one could fix it. The owners hired
a soft-spoken mechanic, with 40 years of experience.
He inspected the engine carefully, top to bottom,
reached into his bag and pulled out a small hammer.
He gently tapped the metal.
Instantly, the engine lurched to life. The engine was
fixed!

Days later, the owner received his bill:
$10,000.
'What?!' he exclaimed. "This is outrageous!" He called
the mechanic, shouting:

"You hardly did anything! Send me an *itemized* bill." Days
later, the owner received a new itemized bill. It read:

— *Tapping with a hammer: $2.*
— *Knowing where to tap: $9,998"*

Do not ever underestimate your own experience!
Your exprience is highly valuable!

Share it! Build yourself and your legacy step by step. Become a mentor for those starting out.

Become a high-ticket expert for your niche market!

Within your family, within organizations and companies, with young professionals, and even within nations.

Live to tell your story and enjoy the journey along the way.

Epilogue

"The only person you are destined to become is the person you decide to be." –Ralph Waldo Emerson

Once you decide to take your life into your own hands, there is no turning back. The freedom, joy, resourcefulness, and fearlessness you experience in having faced and survived it all will stay with you.

Resilience, grit, and perseverance are the backbones of life, which allow you to not only thrive, but to contribute to things bigger than just yourself, making an impact wherever you go and creating change against all odds.

"Here is to the crazy ones, the misfits, the rebels, the trouble-makers, the round pegs in the square holes… the ones who see things differently they are not fond of rules … You can quote them, disagree with them, glorify, or vilify them, but the only thing you cannot do is ignore them, because they change things … they push the human race forward, and while some may see them as the crazy ones, we see genius, because the ones who are crazy enough to think that they can change the world are the ones who do." –Steve Jobs

We are all on this same journey called life, sitting in our own life boat, facing the ups and downs, the waves, and the storms.

Yet there are amazing sunsets, turquoise, and calm waters too.

Enjoy the ride.

Life is all about learning, unlearning, and relearning. *"Wisdom is letting go of something every day."* –Zen

Based on the provided knowledge in this book, you can (re)build and take consistent action toward your goals and achieve them one by one.

Your focus, patience, kindness, and perseverance will pay off big time if you keep on track and do not give up!

Keep going!

You will ever have to make it only through the next one minute at a time!

Keep breathing it is the essence of being alive.

Keep your eyes, ears, and heart open, and notice the beauty of life around you everywhere you go, even in the most unlikely of circumstances and the smallest of things.

Regardless of people and circumstances, you are living and breathing every moment to the fullest, being grateful that this breath is not your last.

Now, what will you do with it?

Appreciation

This book has been written for you based on personal and professional experience around the world.

It is dedicated to all those ambitious enough who strive to overcome often impossible challenges, and who choose to keep becoming and keep going regardless, deciding that life has more to offer than just what happens to them.

We are always only one decision away from a completely different life experience.

I appreciate the ones who strive to become fulfilled and happy; my love goes out to you. It is far easier to sit around, complain, and do nothing.

The doers lift humanity to strive for better one person at a time and let it ripple through.

Thank you for not giving up and carrying your light forward!

My thanks go as well to the international top-level professionals, successful entrepreneurs, and change-makers around the world, who I have had the great honor and pleasure to meet in person or online over the last decades.

I appreciate the time you set aside for our personal talks, feedback, the many inter views, and the exchange of ideas for the creation of this book and my Resilient Power®

approach over the last decade to drive constructive change forward on a large scale.

You have believed that change is possible and each of you contributed a puzzle piece to Resilient Power's® vision and mission, helping to make it a reality.

To this day, it has led to more than 29 international awards and nominations, showing that there is resonance for our work and its outcomes, having created lasting and constructive change around the world.

Success truly is a team sport.

I would further like to thank my many mentors, coaches, advisors, and partners over the decades who catapulted me forward through their teachings and belief in me and my potential to keep growing, granting me their time, knowledge, network, insights, sharing their experiences and their expertise with me. Thank you! My greatest thanks go to my children.

You are my motivation and drive for everything I do. I love you far beyond what words can convey and always will.

May you continue in your own right and ways to create a positive impact in this world.

Continue to create a life that makes you happy, healthy, wealthy, fulfilled, prosperous, and successful.

If someone tells you it can't be done, remember that this means you can't do it with them.

Lasting beauty lies in the light we carry inside out. Plug into the source and let it come through you, not from you.

"'Those who trust in the Lord will renew their strength; they will soar on wings like eagles; they will run and not become weary, they will walk and not faint.'" –Isaiah, 40:31

This verse kept me going over the decades through the darkest of times.

To my family. You have been my steady motivation and inspiration to grow far and beyond my limitations and circumstances, to persevere and create a better life against all odds, not just for ourselves but for others as well.

Without you and who you are, this would never have been possible. You will always be remembered for your grit and resilience in the face of adversities, conquering them the best way you knew how to .

You never gave up.

As my late father always used to say: *"Where there is a will, there is a way."*

"Our deepest fear is not that we are inadequate.

Our deepest fear is that we are powerful beyond measure. It is our light, not our darkness that most frightens us. We ask ourselves, 'Who am I to be brilliant, gorgeous, talented, and fabulous?'

Who are you not to be? You are a child of God. Your playing small does not serve the world. There is nothing enlightened about shrinking so that other people won't feel insecure around you.

We are all meant to shine, as children do. We were born to manifest the glory of God that is within us; it's in everyone.

And as we let our own light shine, we unconsciously give other people permission to do the same.

As we are liberated from our own fear, our presence automatically liberates others."

–Marianne Williamson, *A Return to Love: Reflections on the Principles of "A Course in Miracles"*

Read by Nelson Mandela in his presidency acceptance speech.

Disclaimer

The information in this book is provided for educational and awareness purposes only, sharing experience, and is not intended as medical, financial, or legal advice.

It is meant to be a supportive lifelong compass to provide inputs and guidance towards finding your own answers in your life, culture, situation, and environment.

The content is derived from professional sources believed to be accurate. The information presented and any suggestions expressed, constitute but a guide to further seek appropriate knowledge and facts that apply to your personal and professional circumstances in the country of your residence and legal assets.

The author, hence, does not accept any liability under any circumstances.

Please always consult and seek advice from independent and highly qualified professionals in their respective fields in the place of your legal residence.

**Success starts with strong Self-Leadership!
Ready to step up your game?**

When the rubber hits the road, how exactly do
you create your best possible outcome, rising like
the phoenix out of the ashes?

**In a rapidly changing and complex world, this book guides
you in how to build and engineer your success step by step
to move forward, get ahead, and rise again.**

As a Zen proverb states, only the crystal-clear question
yields a transparent answer.

- How can you stay strong and resilient, and not only persevere but succeed in the face of adversity?
- How do you pull through fears and great challenges?
- How do you make the necessary changes to reach and stay at the top of your game?
- How do you create real change inside out to reach your best possible outcome?
- How do you become and consistently stay successful, making a real impact beyond self?

This book draws out your own answers, insights, and solutions by asking highly relevant, proven, and tested questions concerning The 8 Key Areas in Life.

"The best way to predict your future is to create it."
–Abraham Lincoln

Your choices and actions today leave an impact far beyond just yourself, they are rippling through your environment and generations to come!

To work daily with the international multi-award-winning Resilient Power® App and proprietary The Key 8 Approach, gain access to:

Download **Resilient Power®** Today!

(Self) Leadership Excellence
Engineered from within:

- International Award-winning
- Proprietary Methodology
- Proven Strategies
- Effective Frameworks
- Measurable Results

Download on the **App Store**

GET IT ON **Google Play**

Awards & Achievements (Selection)

- Sustainability Champion Award
- Global HOPE Award
- Microsoft Startup Founder Hub (only 1%-3% global acceptance rate)
- Most Innovative Startups GenAIFund in Productivity & Business Solutions
- Nominee Singapore Business Review Technology Excellence Awards: Nominated as one of Singapore's Leading Companies in Technological Innovation

About the Author

Sharesz T. Wilkinson is a globally acclaimed award-winning thought leader, change maker, and leadership expert. As Founder and CEO of Resilient Power®, based in Singapore, she combines resilience engineering with cutting-edge technology, ethical impact, top-level executive communication, and personal branding to empower leaders worldwide.

A sought-after keynote speaker and board advisor, Sharesz has worked with Stanford LEAD, Fortune 200 executives, and top global events. Her proprietary, science-based approach helps leaders and teams build authentic connections, self-leadership, and resilience to achieve their goals during challenging times.

She contributes as a member of the Singapore Mentorship Committee, as an international startup judge, and mentor for the National University Singapore Entrepreneurship Society. Sharesz is also a founder alumnus of Microsoft Startup Founder Hub and a global Venture Partner, maintaining strong ties to Silicon Valley.

Her co-authored book *Success Mindsets* (Simon & Schuster) topped Amazon's Entrepreneurship category and appeared on The Wall Street Journal and USA Today bestseller lists. Widely featured in Forbes, BBC, and NBC, Sharesz draws on her diverse expertise in executive mentoring, crisis management, and entrepreneurship to inspire others to build lasting resilient power amid rapid global change.

She has dedicated herself over the decades to create change top-down one leader and their team at a time, letting it ripple through companies, organizations, and entire nations.

For latest updates and contact details, please see: https:// linktr.ee/stwilkinson, for collaborations and keynotes, please contact: admin@resilientpower.global